W9-AIB-545

WHAT PEOPLE ARE SAYING
ABOUT THIS BOOK

As Elvis might have said: "A hunka-hunka burnin' history!" Truly *riiiiipped* from headlines of Texas history, mystery, legend, lore, gore, nighttime rainbows, and more...this is quite a read!

Betcha-can't-read-just-one...no way, gotta read them all, these often jaw-dropping gems of flabbergast. If I were an elementary school teacher, I'd read one of these a day aloud in class to spice up social studies and prove that the truth (at least according to Texas media) is stranger than...well, almost everything. Let's hope there's a sequel!

—Carole Marsh, author of *The Alamo Ghost, The Cowboy Christmas Ball,* and *Hard-to-Believe-But-True Facts About Texas*

In this volume Chad Lewis proves there are reaches of darkness, territories of the unknown, and hidden ghost stories that most readers are not familiar with. Chad includes obscure tales that only the most serious of occult scholars will have seen before.

However, this book does not confine itself to frightening tales collected from mysterious texts. Chad adds his own insights and theories of the citing ghost stories dating as far back as 1860. Written in a fashion that is not only fun to read but is also academic and reader friendly. This is a book that will edify as well as terrify.

—Rene Bleys, Parapsychologist of The Paranormal Research Society of Texas

HIDDEN
HEADLINES
OF

TEXAS

Strange, Unusual, & Bizarre Newspaper Stories
1860-1910

HIDDEN HEADLINES
OF
TEXAS

Strange, Unusual, & Bizarre Newspaper Stories
1860-1910

Researched and Compiled by
Chad Lewis

Foreword by Nick Redfern

Research Publishing Company
A Division of Unexplained Research, LLC

Library of Congress Control Number: 2007928698
ISBN-10: 0-9762099-8-5
ISBN-13: 978-0-9762099-8-0

Printed in the United States by Documation

Unexplained Research Publishing Company
A Division of Unexplained Research LLC
P.O. Box 2173, Eau Claire, WI 54702-2173
Email: info@unexplainedresearch.com
www.unexplainedresearch.com

Cover Design: Jeannine & Terry Fisk
Illustrations: Rick Fisk
Portrait: Rob Mattison

DEDICATION

This book is dedicated to the loving memory of
Sean Lewis,
who left our world much too soon.

TABLE OF CONTENTS

FOREWORD
by
Nick Redfern

Although British by birth, I have lived in Texas for six years, and for the last four of those, specifically in the city of Dallas. And, as someone who has personally investigated a whole range of mysterious events, alien encounters and monstrous stories that originated deep within the heart of the Lone Star State, when Chad Lewis (co-author with Terry Fisk of *The Minnesota Road Guide to Haunted Locations*) asked me if I would write the foreword to his new book, *Hidden Headlines of Texas*, I didn't even have to think twice.

The theme of the book is a very interesting one. As you may well deduce from its title, *Hidden Headlines* is an in-depth study of an absolute plethora of tales on all things eerie, paranormal, bizarre and macabre that have found their way into the many and varied newspapers of Texas.

But what makes the book particularly notable is the fact that Chad has focused specifically on the period from 1860 to 1910. And for this he is to be applauded. Whereas securing the latest, breaking news from today's worlds of Ufology, Cryptozoology and Ghost-Hunting in Texas requires little more than an Internet connection and a decent search-engine, delving back to a period in American history that is long gone is a somewhat more difficult and arduous task.

So, in other words, for those fans of the unexplained who want to know all about the high-strangeness that dominated the lives of the people of Texas more than a century ago—as well as learning about those stories that would otherwise be utterly lost to the fog of time—*Hidden Headlines* is a title that you cannot afford to miss. And what, you may ask, will you find within the packed pages of Chad's title? Well, the answer is plenty, I am pleased to say.

The book is split into a number of sections that cover such wide-ranging issues as UFOs, strange creatures, bizarre deaths, ghosts and the paranormal, medical anomalies, and more. And I have to say that I was truly amazed at the sheer scale of absolute weirdness that abounded throughout the entire state in the 50-year period that *Hidden Headlines* covers.

Strange suicides, apparent corpses rising from the grave, and the odd story of the woman who laughed herself to death are just the mere beginning. For those that thrill to tales of all-things spooky, you will find much entertainment in the stories of the haunted piano, the voodoo priest of Springtown, the ghostly child of Dallas' Watkins Hotel, and even the very weird saga of the bicycle-riding specter.

And, as the book makes very clear, Texas of the mid-to-late nineteenth century was packed with some very strange and unusual looking characters that would have been quite at home on the set of the movie *Deliverance*. Indeed, Chad introduces us to the family from Cisco that could practically all boast of possessing an extra finger on each hand, the African-American man who turned white (no, his name was not Michael Jackson…), the San Antonio resident who was neither male nor female (or was "it" a combination of both?), the diabolical baby of Weatherford that was reported as being part-human, part-pig, and part-elephant, and a strange creature described by journalists as a combination of human-being and centipede! Undoubtedly, these two latter stories had their origins in tales of tragic—and, at the time, poorly understood—human deformity rather than anything stranger. Yet, it is instructive and illuminating to see how the media reported on such issues back then.

And the animals of Texas were a weird bunch, too. There was the mystery puma of Whitewright, a seven-legged calf, the 40-foot-long tapeworm removed from a child's stomach, the shaggy Wildman of the San Antonio River, giant eagles, a ten-horned cow, and the pig-baby of Groesbeck.

Then there are those stories that are just plain odd, such as that of the tree without a trunk that thrived very nicely while suspended a number of feet above the ground. And what are we to make of the graveyard that was a home not to dead bodies, but rather to just body parts—such as legs and fingers? I will let you find the answer to that riddle for yourself. And how many people knew that Texas had its own equivalent of the Great Wall of China? Or that at least one resident of the Lone Star State outgrew his own coffin? I know they say that everything is bigger in Texas, but that's taking things to ridiculous proportions!

Perhaps I should also mention the Waco Hermit, the one-eyed wild-woman of Terrell, and Beaumont's "Baby Jim," who weighed in at a whopping 750 pounds, and for whom the words "I'll have my order super-sized" were surely made.

Cryptozoology, UFOs, and psychic phenomena all feature heavily too in *Hidden Headlines*, with much attention given to stories of séances, clairvoyance, hypnotism, premonitions of death, ball-lightning, the mysterious airship invasion and the alleged "UFO crash" at the sleepy little town of Aurora in 1897; a nighttime rainbow, sea-serpents, giant marauding wolves, and much, much more.

This is one of those books that is a real joy to read and one that transports the reader back to a time very different to that of today, and where wonders and marvels of a distinctly strange kind abounded on what seems to have been practically a daily basis.

You don't have to live in Texas to enjoy and appreciate Chad's book. You just need to have a love and appreciation of the unexplained, the bizarre, the mysterious, and (at times) the down-right ridiculous and the surreal.

A stranger and more entertaining view of old Texas, you will not find. Not just recommended reading, *Hidden Headlines* is essential reading.

Nick Redfern is the author of many books on the paranormal and unsolved mysteries, including *Three Men Seeking Monsters, Strange Secrets,* and *Memoirs of a Monster Hunter.*

Introduction

Texas is a really big place, with plenty of room for its 23 million people to stretch out, explore, and of course, plenty of room to experience the weird. A lot of things have changed in the last 150 years. This is especially true when you consider that in 1860, the population of the state was just over 600,000 people.

When you look back at how people lived, worked, traveled, and played, it seems like they were living in a completely different world. Most of us believe that those who lived 100 years ago were well grounded, rational, more conservative, and possessed greater common sense than we do today. Their world moved at a slower pace, seemed less chaotic, and provided time to reflect on the important issues of the day.

People 100 years ago would not have sat home watching reality TV; they would have been too busy chasing the local "wild man" that was terrorizing their town. There would have been no time for text messaging friends, as you would be too busy grabbing your fishing pole in hopes of landing the giant sea serpent that had been spotted in the lake. Playing video games was out of the question as long as the town was frenzied over the ghostly happenings taking place at the haunted farm. The sky wasn't filled with smog, it was littered with strange lights and crashing ships. Neighbors were not strangers; they were the people who brought over the animal that was part pig, part elephant and part human for you to see.

Unfortunately, the good old days are gone, and no wishing will ever bring them back. Yet these stories provide a rare opportunity to vicariously experience what it was like to be a resident living in early Texas. Allow yourself to be transported back to a time long since past, but be prepared—the newspapers of old were not quite like those of today. The style of writing, along with the spattering of aged words may appear a bit old fashioned and archaic to you, but, if you let it, this "old" type of writing will make you feel like you just picked today's newspaper off your front porch. Readers may also be shocked by some of the language that is outright sexist, racist, and bigoted. To accurately present these stories in their historical context, I have not censored or changed any of the writing or wording.

The papers also tended to cover a story in a manner that often left the reader with many unanswered questions. What ever happened to the human fish? Was that town haunting ever solved? Did the residents ever find the mysterious object that crashed into the ground? These and many more questions are left for you to speculate on, or perhaps even solve.

Of course, as a modern reader with a current perspective, you may undoubtedly look at these cases and wonder if someone listed as "dying of fright" actually died of a heart attack while they were frightened. You may also wonder whether that "wild man" with long black body hair that was spotted roaming the woods was actually a Bigfoot, or that just maybe that "hovering meteor" was really a UFO. You will also see I have not made any judgment as to the validity of these cases and I have refrained from telling you whether or not I even believe them. I have simply presented them to you as exactly the way you would have read them on the day they were printed.

Regardless of what conclusions you come to after reading this book, I am certain that these Texas stories will provide you a glimpse of the state in its simpler, slower-paced, and much, much weirder past.

Enjoy the adventure,

Chad Lewis

ACKNOWLEDGMENTS

I would like to thank Nick Redfern, Nisa Giaquinto, Sarah Szymanski, Rob Mattison, Rick Fisk, Jeannine Fisk, and Terry Fisk for assisting with the research and production of this book.

HIDDEN HEADLINES of TEXAS

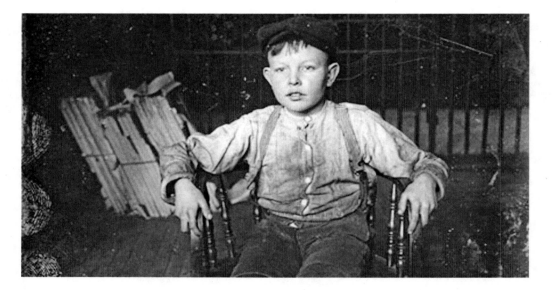

From Hempstead

HEMPSTEAD- Dr. N.H. Hunter, dentist, dropped dead, while extracting the tooth of a patient, this evening.

—*The Galveston Daily News*
April 14, 1875

❖ ❖ ❖

Lemonade Death

WEATHERFORD- A man by the name of John Palmer dropped dead at Weatherford, in this state, a few days ago, from drinking three glasses of that non-intoxicating beverage—lemonade. The enemies of cold water and similar sedative will not fail to turn this incident to the promotion of their cause. They will call attention to the frequency with which the harvest hand drops dead after imbibing a swig of ice water while he, not the swig, is in a heated condition. They will say we never read of a man falling dead while quietly sucking a mint julep through a straw, while all manner of danger lurks in the glass of lemonade. They will tell you how witnesses proudly testify in court that they drink sixty, seventy, and even more glasses of beer a day, and keep right on acquiring adipose tissue and high social status, while the man who gulps down a glass of lemonade is in danger of being summoned hence immediately and so on.

—*The Galveston Daily News*
September 19, 1879

❖ ❖ ❖

EXTRA! EXTRA!

In 1900, the average life expectancy was 47 years.

Found Dead In Graveyard

Mr. Daniel Bell, Of Akard Street. Worn Out And Broken Down By Consumption Retires To The Old Catholic Cemetery And Takes His Life.

DALLAS- Yesterday morning the dead body of Daniel Bell was found in the old Catholic cemetery, and close by it was an envelope marked "morphine," which explained the cause of death. The deceased was 43 years old and resided in Akard Street with his family, in indigent circumstances. He had been suffering from tubercular consumption for five years, and of late had grown too weak for physical exertion. This seemed to weigh heavily on his mind, and he gradually grew tired of life. For some time previous to his death he had made frequent visits to the cemetery, where he would stay by the hour, evidently engaged in contemplation of that relief which was only to be found at the grave. The happiest relations seemed to have existed between him and his family, and his inability to assist and serve those most dear to him was undoubtedly the rock upon which his mind was shattered. A jury of inquest was summoned by Justice Schuhl and the following proceedings had:

The Inquest

Justice Schuhl, acting coroner, impaneled a jury of inquest, and the following testimony was adduced:

Mrs. Lucy Bell

Wife of the deceased, was first sworn, and testified as follows: I am the wife of deceased; we had been married fourteen years; saw him last time yesterday about 6:30 p.m. as he was getting out of bed; been ailing during the day; he got up to get something for the children's supper, as I was sick myself. On leaving he said to Lillia, my little daughter, that he would be back in a little while. Within the last week he has been found in the cemetery two or three times, from whence I got him during the night. He seemed to have a fancy for sleeping there and has been for the past five years failing with consumption, and of late, at times, acted very strange, as if partly out of his mind. For example, he would suppose that he was not doing his duty towards his family, and again that he himself was neglected. As for myself, I feel satisfied that no cause existed why the act was committed, unless it be extreme weakness and sudden loss of mind. For the last five weeks I have watched him nightly, on account of his coughing spells, for fear that he would strangle. He never wanted any physician. Dr. Thurston knew his condition, he having attended him three months ago, when he met with an accident. He never took morphine. In fact he abhorred it. He was 43 years old.

A. Birklein

I live about one square from the home of the deceased. I knew him. I know nothing of the cause, except his strange actions yesterday about 8 o'clock, when he did not appear rational. For instance, he jumped over the fence while the gate was open, though he was crippled, and ran over to the old Catholic cemetery.

Verdict

The jury returned the following verdict: We, the jury impaneled and sworn to investigate the cause and the manner of the death of Daniel Bell, find that an overdose of morphine was the cause, which was administered by himself with suicidal intent, caused from a deranged mind.
G.W. McCormick,
F.W. Wheless,
W.R. Jones,
H.S. Calbreath,
D.C. Dunlap,
Jno. P. Roberts.

—*Dallas Morning News*
June 17, 1886

❖ ❖ ❖

Killed By The Falling Of A Tree

GALVESTON- During a wind storm at Far Plains, Panola County, to-day, a tree was blown down, crushing the residence of Mrs. Watkins and instantly killed her sis-ter, Mrs. Albert Little and her two small children.

—*The Memphis Daily Avalanche*
June 23, 1887

❖ ❖ ❖

A Lady Frightened To Death

MARSHALL- Mrs. Cassie Jackson, wife of Rev. J.H. Jackson, was alarmed by a man, who had been working for her husband, entering the yard of her residence in a drunken condition and going to the house as if to walk in. A short time after Mrs. Jackson swooned and fell to the ground, and was carried in the house. Medical aid was called, but she expired an hour later. The cause of death is thought to have been congestion of the lungs and brain, aggravated by the fright.

—*Dallas Morning News*
December 15, 1887

Died

GARRETT- A young man named Dalman living near Garrett, Lamar County, ate some May apples while out hunting. Soon afterwards he was taken sick and died in about two hours.

—*Rockdale Messenger*
July 4, 1889

❖ ❖ ❖

Dropped Dead While Drinking Water

SAN ANTONIO- C.O. Herring, a stranger quartered at the Southern Hotel, fell dead this morning when in the act of taking a drink from a glass of water. He had heart disease. It was reported that he had poisoned himself, but the inquest developed that there was no foundation for the sensational rumor and the coroner rendered a verdict of death from natural causes.

—*The Galveston Daily News*
September 21, 1891

❖ ❖ ❖

Dragged To Death

HENRIETTA- Marvin Ozee, son of J.M. Ozee, one of the old settlers of this county, was thrown from his horse yesterday morning while trying to rope a cow, and becoming entangled in the rope was dragged to death by the horse, which was young and wild. He was still alive when found, but died at 3 o'clock this morning.

—*Fort Worth Gazette*
September 14, 1893

❖ ❖ ❖

A Sweetheart Dies Nursing Her Lover
He Suicides

CORPUS CHRISTI- Some three or four months ago Leonires Gomez, who lived about twenty miles from town, mysteriously disappeared. For several years past, prior to his disappearance, Gomez had been afflicted with a terrible disease which was beyond the ken of the physicians. At times he suffered intensely and from it he became a hideous looking man. When he was first taken down he was engaged to a pretty Mexican girl who waited at his bedside during his illness until she fell a victim to the dreaded disease and died from its effects. Her death created a deep impression on Gomez, and he told his friends he, too, would soon be out of trouble. That night he disappeared, and though his friends instituted a vigorous search, it was not until yesterday that their efforts were rewarded. Gomez, it seems, had wandered out in the brush a mile or so from where he lived and had there taken his own life with a knife which was found near the body. The body was reduced to a mere skeleton when discovered as was identified by the clothes Gomez wore.

—*Fort Worth Gazette*
November 10, 1894

❖ ❖ ❖

Peculiar Death

OAK CLIFF- A most peculiar death occurred in Oak Cliff last night. Fire broke out in the residence of Mrs. Josie A. Sutter, corner of Eighth and Greenwood Streets. Al Perkins, one of the Oak Cliff volunteer firemen, started to give the alarm, when he dropped dead. The house burned down, and in the rush it was some little time before it was realized that Perkins was dead. Medical aid was instantly summoned and when the doctor arrived Perkins was pronounced dead. An inquest was held this morning on the remains. The cause of the death is attributed to heart disease. Perkins' friends say he was subject to slight attacks occasionally. The house that burned was valued at $1000, and was insured for $1000.

—*Fort Worth Gazette*
December 9, 1894

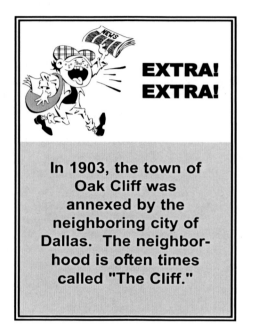

EXTRA! EXTRA!

In 1903, the town of Oak Cliff was annexed by the neighboring city of Dallas. The neighborhood is often times called "The Cliff."

Dead Man Came To Life
A Supposed Corpse Revives And Then Goes And Dies Again

GALVESTON- The coroner and the undertaker were almost cheated out of a job to-night. Along about 6:30 Joe Praker telephoned the police station from the extreme west end of the city that a dead man was lying at Fifty-seventh Street and the beach. The police telephoned J. Levy & Bros., who sent their wagon and Undertaker Norwood to the scene. Sergeant Delaya, Special Officers Duffy and Amundsen and Coroner Barry went out in separate conveyances.

When they reached the spot something like a half hour afterward they found an old man lying with his face in the sand, his hands over his abdomen and his body bent as if he was suffering from cramps. They put him in the temporary coffin, known to the profession as "the box," and brought him to town. Life seemed extinct, although one man said that when they straightened out the body he noticed a puffing out of the cheeks, followed by a return to a natural position. He was stiff and cold and to all appearances dead.

When they got him out of his wet clothes and onto the cooling board it was noticed that there was more of that puffing of the cheeks. Norwood pulled back his eyelids, "Why, this man is not dead. Go for a doctor." The colored boys about the stable, who had stood in awe of death, scampered at the announcement of the resurrection and went into the office where it was light and warm. Somebody went for a doctor, who arrived in about eight minutes. As soon as life was discovered, the officers and others commenced to rub the body with spirits. The physician, upon his arrival, applied the electric battery, hot bricks were put at the extremities and hips and the body kept as warm as possible. It was not so very long before the old man began to breathe heavily, and though the process of resuscitation was slow, he gradually revived.

When found he wore no overcoat, but was well enough clad otherwise. He wore an indigo blue coat, gray vest, white shirt, heavy red flannel undergarments, dark trousers, red socks and leather slippers. By his side was a sack of red apples. He had evidently been out in the rain most of the day, as his clothes were completely wet through. In the pockets were found $1.05 in small change, a pocket knife, a bit of lead pencil and a couple pieces of paper, on one of which was written with a lead pencil, "Physeanthus Belle," and on the other, "Bon Silene," "Carmen Shadede," "The Bride," "Celin Forster." The opinion was expressed that these might be the names of flowers and he a gardener. He was not identified up to a late hour this evening. In appearance he is a tall man with red hair that sticks up around a bald spot, and red whiskers, both of which were sprinkled with gray. Someone working about the man said that his name was Edwards, but as this could not be corroborated and the person making the statement was not sure, his identity is still clouded.

At 10:30 o'clock the man died, after having shown evidences of coming to life. He did not fully recover consciousness. The physician who attended him said that he believed he had taken an opiate of some kind.

—*Dallas Morning News*
December 30, 1895

❖ ❖ ❖

EXTRA! EXTRA!

The fear of being buried alive was so prevalent that devices were invented and patented to insure a safe burial. One strange device was a spring-loaded casket lid that could be opened by the slightest movement from inside the coffin.

Died On Her Wedding Day
A Pathetic Story Told A News Reporter Yesterday

DALLAS- On Tuesday morning a young farmer named W.P. Milles, who resides in the Seagoville neighborhood, was in the city and called at the office of the county clerk and said to Mr. Henry Skelton, the deputy clerk: "I want a marriage license. To-morrow I shall wed Miss S.M. Wilkinson. We have been engaged for several months and March 17th has been selected as the happy day. On Saturday last my intended was stricken down. A physician pronounced it a case of diphtheria. This morning he said to me: "I have the case under control, the young lady is convalescing and you need not postpone the wedding."

Mr. Mills secured the license and went on his way rejoicing. Yesterday afternoon he returned to Dallas and called at the office of the county clerk again. Pulling a document from his pocket he handed it to Mr. Skelton, saying while the tears ran down his cheeks, "I have no use for this now. Miss Wilkerson, who was to have become my wife to-day died this morning. It is a funeral instead of a wedding and I am in Dallas to select a coffin for my intended bride." His voice was trembling with emotion and if ever a man exhibited a feeling of profound grief it was this broken-hearted young farmer whose loved one had exchanged a bridal robe for a shroud.

—*Dallas Morning News*
March 18, 1897

❖ ❖ ❖

Two Remarkable Coincidences
A Son Suicides Where His Father Did.
A Son Breaks His Thigh Where His Father Did.

ORANGE- About 8 o'clock this morning, George Beauchamp, 22 years old, unmarried, rode over to the home of his brother-in-law, J. Mulvey, went into the house, sat down and talked with the family for a few minutes, apparently in the best of spirits.

He then stepped into an unoccupied room and before any one suspected his intention, drew a pistol and shot himself through the head.

The family rushed in, but he died instantly. No cause for the rash act can be divined by those who knew him. He was a promising young farmer, industrious and honorable. Less than two years ago young Beauchamp's father committed suicide by shooting himself near the same locality.

Just before 3 o'clock this afternoon Olive Harmen was driving along the road not far from Terry, when his horse took fright, ran away, dashed the buggy against a tree, throwing Harmen out and in falling he struck against a stump, broke his left thigh bone and bruised his whole body badly. Strangely enough John Harmen, father of the young man mentioned above, was driving a pair of oxen attached to a cart along the same road less than a year ago, when they became unruly, ran into the woods, upset the cart, threw the old gentleman out and in falling across a log, broke his thigh bone.

—*Dallas Morning News*
June 20, 1897

❖ ❖ ❖

A Strange Coincidence
Young Man And His Fiancé Die At The Same Time

BONHAM- A strange occurrence happened at Lannius, seven miles north of here last week. A young man and Miss Lankford, both of said community were to have been married last Friday. A few days previous to the time set for the wedding the young man was stricken with the fever and lived until Thursday. On Thursday of last week his intended bride was thrown from a horse and sustained serious injuries from which she died in a few hours. The two were buried at the New Prospect cemetery on Friday, the day set for the wedding.

—*Dallas Morning News*
August 30, 1898

Dropped Dead

EL PASO- A young man was stricken with a hemorrhage of the lungs while standing on a prominent corner to-day. He made his way into a saloon and asked for a glass of whiskey. It was given him, and immediately after swallowing the contents of the glass he dropped dead. His name was Edward Apodiea.

—*The Galveston Daily News*
November 18, 1898

Odd Accident

SEALY- John Oldog, a young German farmer living about five miles south met with an accident Thursday that cost him his life. While returning from hunting with his son, his buggy hit a rut and the child was thrown out and the father, while trying to catch the child, dropped the gun and it discharged, striking him in the abdomen. He lingered until Friday night. A wife and four small children survive.

—*Rockdale Messenger*
December 8, 1898

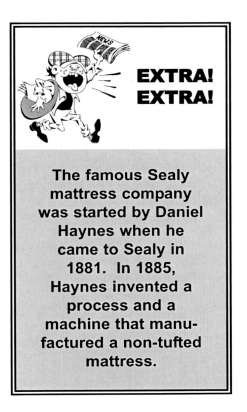

EXTRA! EXTRA!

The famous Sealy mattress company was started by Daniel Haynes when he came to Sealy in 1881. In 1885, Haynes invented a process and a machine that manufactured a non-tufted mattress.

Lady Ate Glass And Died

GATESVILLE- Mrs. David Taffinder, who was adjudged insane on the 17th instant here and was taken home under bond to await transfer to the asylum died suddenly at her home in Oglesby a few days ago from eating glass.

—*Dallas Morning News*
January 25, 1899

❖ ❖ ❖

Death At Funeral

TEXARKANA- Ed Marshall, a Texarkana young man, was taken sick and died while attending the funeral of a niece at that city.

—*Rockdale Messenger*
February 9, 1899

❖ ❖ ❖

Strange Fatality

EAGLE PASS- On the 10th instant, Charles Carter of this county died in Eagle Pass of asthma. His brother George Carter, age 68, was prostrated by the loss of his brother and one week later he died. A sister, Miss Anniette Carter, overcome by grief at the loss of her two brothers, took to bed and died four days later. The Carters were old settlers of Maverick County.

—*Rockdale Messenger*
March 2, 1899

❖ ❖ ❖

A Strange Reappearance

HOUSTON- Israel Branch, a negro, returned home after an absence of two years, this morning, for the first time. He staggered into the house in a maudlin condition. His mother attempted to arouse him, but he mumbled incoherently and then dropped dead. Deceased's face was horribly discolored, exhibiting unmistakable signs of poison. Justice Malsch is sifting the affair.

—*San Antonio Daily Light*
September 24, 1899

❖ ❖ ❖

Bullet Through Heart
A. Blenker Took His Own Life In A Cemetery Sitting On A Bench In Front Of The Famous King Monument. He Committed The Death In A Very Cool Manner.

SAN ANTONIO- Sitting on an iron bench at the base of the King monument in City Cemetery No. 4, between two graves, the body of A. Blenker was found cold and stiff this morning at 6:30 o'clock, a bullet hole in the breast over the heart and other evidences plainly telling the history of the tragic death.

The body was found by a little son of lawyer F.L. Ripley as he was passing through and he at once ran to No. 6 fire engine house half a block away and informed Captain Miller of his ghastly find. The Captain notified the police and coroner and Mounted Officers Herroca and Parker were soon on the scene.

The officers and others who had gathered soon learned the identity of the man by papers left by him. A .45 caliber pistol with one chamber empty lay a couple of feet in front of the dead body, which was stiff, and to the weapon was attached a tag with the words "Pistol is property of A.B. Frank & Co." written thereon. An empty chamber in the weapon and a bullet hole over the heart explained to what purpose it had been used.

Beside the man on the iron bench lay his overcoat carefully folded, to which was attached a note which read as follows: "Ring up 75G, two rings, Ben Nentwig."

—*San Antonio Daily Light*
January 2, 1900

❖ ❖ ❖

Died On The Train
On The Way To San Antonio For His Health.
Sad End Of William Sherrell Atkinson Of Tennessee.

HOUSTON- William Sherrell Atkinson, aged 31, died on the Southern Pacific passenger train coming from the east this morning. He was on his way to San Antonio from Maxwell, Tenn., accompanied by his wife for the benefit of his health, and occupied a berth in a tourist sleeper. At Houston a doctor attended him and pronounced him in the last stages of consumption. He died at Rosenberg at 1:12 o'clock this morning. The remains were brought to San Antonio and Coroner Sweeney held an inquest. Undertakers J.T. Burnett & Co., prepared the body for burial and shipped it to Fayetteville, Tenn., this afternoon, accompanied by the wife of the deceased.

—*San Antonio Daily Light*
February 8, 1900

❖ ❖ ❖

Died Of Joy
Eliza Nelson Had Prepared A Pleasant Surprise.
She Was To Have Left For Beeville To-day On A Visit To Her Grandchildren And Was Carried Away With Heart Disease.

SAN ANTONIO- In joyful celebration of a visit to her grandchildren in Beeville, Eliza Nelson, a well known colored auntie of the city, sank to the ground last night lifeless. She was a cook in the family of T.B. Johnson, at West End, and was on her way home at 1148 Menchien Street to pick up her things for the trip when she suffered a stroke of heart disease. She had intended to leave and had made preparations for a few little surprises for her grandchildren upon her arrival at Beeville. Deceased had been in the employ of Mr. Johnson's family the past fifteen years, and was always faithful and prompt in attending in her duties.

—*San Antonio Daily Light*
February 24, 1900

❖ ❖ ❖

Cause Of The Tragedy

CROCKETT- Yesterday about 30 miles north of here, Jim Barrow was shot and instantly killed by John Hearn. Mrs. Hearn was so shocked by the tragedy that she dropped dead almost as soon as Barrow was shot. The cause of the killing was that Hearn objected to Barrow's attention to his young daughter.

—*The Galveston Daily News*
March 18, 1902

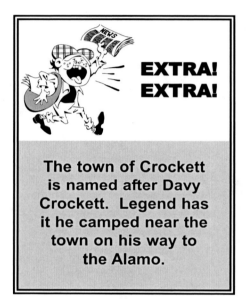

The town of Crockett is named after Davy Crockett. Legend has it he camped near the town on his way to the Alamo.

Aged Pair Die Together
Lived Fifty-Six Years As Man And Wife And Had 25 Children

BROWNSVILLE- Two deaths have occurred here within the past twenty-four hours that bring to light something out of the ordinary. Santana Cortina and his wife have been married fifty-six years, and during this period twenty-five children have been born of the union, only two of who are still living. Yesterday at 6 o'clock

Cortina died, and this morning his aged wife also passed away at the family residence in the city.

—*The Galveston Daily News*
March 24, 1905

❖ ❖ ❖

Coincidence Of Two Deaths
Brothers Die Same Afternoon And Another May Not Live

FORT WORTH- The death of W.J. McFarland at St. Joseph's Infirmary yesterday afternoon at 1 o'clock brings to light a strange coincidence. At 6 o'clock last night Mr. McFarland's brother, Robert McFarland, died at his home at Chandler, Henderson County. Another brother is in a sanitarium at Dallas and is not expected to live. The McFarland family is well known here and is one of the oldest in East Texas. The remains of W.J. McFarland were shipped to Tyler this morning.

—*Dallas Morning News*
April 20, 1907

❖ ❖ ❖

Found Dead On Father's Grave

AUSTIN- Charles Allen, aged 25 years, who had been employed as a salesman frequently in the last few years by San Antonio wholesale houses, was found dead late this afternoon, lying on his father's grave in the City Cemetery. A 45-caliber revolver lay by his side and a bullet wound had been inflicted in his temple.

The body was discovered, immediately after the sound of the pistol's discharge, by one of the cemetery watchmen. Justice of the Peace J.D. Moore was summoned and rendered a decision of death in accordance with the known facts of the incident. The cemetery watchman had seen Allen enter the graveyard, proceed to his father's grave and sit down by it. Deceased leaves a mother, two sisters and two small brothers.

—*Dallas Morning News*
July 3, 1907

Austin is the live music capital of the world.

Coincidence In Death Of Father And Son

SHERMAN- It is a strange coincidence that Arthur Temple, a young man who was called from Sherman to Wyoming by the accidental death of his father, himself met death on the home ranch early this week in the same manner as his father did by being thrown from a horse. Information came in a letter to friends of the young man in Sherman.

—*Dallas Morning News*
October 10, 1909

The world's first rodeo was held in Pecos on July 4, 1883.

Apologized To Coroner
Man In El Paso Willed Body To Scientists, Wrote Letter To Coroner, And Then Killed Himself.

EL PASO- After writing a will bequeathing his body to medical scientists, and apologizing to the coroner for the trouble he was about to give him, Gus Schell shot himself to death in his room at a South El Paso hotel to-day. Schell was about 50 years of age, and came here from Kansas City, as a government meat inspector, resigning two months ago.

—*The Galveston Daily News*
January 1, 1910

Boy Drops Dead
Jesse Millhanks
Falls On The Street.
His Brother Recently Died
Very Suddenly.

HOUSTON- Jesse Millhanks, aged 14, brother of Charles Millhanks, the youth who dropped dead while at study in the Fulton School on April 18 of last year, suddenly dropped dead this morning as he was walking with his father near his home, at 72 Schrimp's Alley in the Second Ward.

The father and son were on their way home, and were only a short distance from the house when the young man fell dead at his father's feet. The inquest was held by Judge McDonald, who rendered a verdict that death resulted from natural causes. The funeral will be held at 10 o'clock Tuesday morning from the undertaking parlors of C.J. Wright & Co.

—*The Galveston Daily News*
October 4, 1910

❖ ❖ ❖

Died After Being Called Upon To Pray

CENTER- Mandy Holland, an old negro woman was called on by the preacher at the colored Baptist Church last night to offer prayer, and after having begun her prayer her voice became inaudible and investigation being made, the fact was discovered that she was dying. She expired within ten minutes after she was requested to pray.

—*The Galveston Daily News*
November 2, 1910

Ghosts

Unearthly Music

GALVESTON- A haunted house has been discovered in the eastern portion of the city recently. Unearthly music occasionally floats from an unopened piano; empty rooms resound with wild noise; the gas is suddenly extinguished, and other absurd pranks played by the frolicsome ghosts.

—*The Galveston Daily News*
July 12, 1874

❖ ❖ ❖

Moves Out

GALVESTON- The man who rented a haunted house was seen to leave it late one night last week. He was thinly clad at the time.

—*The Galveston Daily News*
March 16, 1875

❖ ❖ ❖

Taylorville's Ghost
The Christian County Ghost
Again Gets His Work In

JOHNSON- The Johnson Township, Christian County, is again called on to do a sensational service. A correspondent of the *Globe-Democrat* writes concerning it, and states that at times the ghost seems in good spirits, and trips over the floor in the gayest manner. He taps on the window pane, rattles the doors, and thumps the walls as if in great anger, and now he groans in agony, making hideous and unearthly noises that are thrilling in the extreme. The signs of distress are described as being like the groans of a horse in great agony. This sort of procedure had been going on for nine years. Family after family have lived there, but none have remained there any great length of time. Each has gone there with the determination to live down superstition, but the strongest resolutions have given way after a short experience in the dismal place.

Various theories as to the cause of these mysterious sounds have been advanced, but each have been abundantly proved unfounded. Everything possible has been done to ferret the mystery, but it remains as much a mystery to-day as ever, and the most incredulous and even-balanced minds in the neighborhood have given way to the belief that there must be "something to it."

The last family that resided there (and they left last week) was that of Samuel Laughlin. They have lived there longer than any of the others, but while they went there entirely free from superstition, they are now firm believers that restless spirits walk on earth and frequent the places where dark and bloody deeds have been done. At first they paid no attention to the noises, but during the last few months, the noises have become more frequent and hideous, until one night last week they became unbearable, and with fear and trembling the terrified family fled from the place. The hired man left some time ago, and he described the groans as being of a most dreadful character, issuing from all parts of the house, but neither he nor anybody else have ever seen a spectral form or ghostly apparition, every attempt to discover the author of the mysterious sounds, which only occur near midnight, proving futile.

The desertion of the house by the Laughlin family has thrown the neighborhood into the wildest excitement. The people say the mystery must be laid bare if the place has to be torn to splinters. Many attribute the mysterious sounds to the fact that many years ago a dastardly murder and robbery is supposed to have been committed there. It is said that a peddler once visited those parts, disposing of many articles to the farmers. He is known to have been in possession of considerable money, and to have had many valuable articles in his pack. He was seen it is said, to enter that house, and none in the vicinity ever saw or heard of him afterward. Foul play was suspected at the time, and as years have passed the suspicion has increased. A few years after the supposed murder a gang of counterfeiters was detected making spurious coin in the house, and it is argued that no doubt many a foul and bloody deed has been committed there. The flight of the Laughlin family tends to more firmly establish this belief, and many discussions of the matter have taken place within the last few days.

—*The Galveston Daily News*
February 10, 1880

All Houses Are Haunted

MARSHALL- "All houses in which men have lived and died are haunted," says the poet, and he only expresses the faith of the ignorant and superstitious. The Herald tells of a haunted house at Marshall where

"no exorcism," even that of hard facts, seems sufficient to bind the restless spirit which, like the pestilence, walks at night.

—*The Galveston Daily News*
June 1, 1884

❖ ❖ ❖

A Haunted House

DALLAS- The Dallas Times had another story of a haunted house. "All homes in which men have lived and died are haunted," says Hood. The Dallas domicile stands alone out on the prairie: "Its lonely situation and dead white color gave it a rather spookish appearance and in the twilight it loomed up as a veritable castle of departed spirits." Strange noises, dim lights, and flitting shadows in the lonely building around the superstitious fears of people and the police were finally called in to exorcise the evil spirits. They "pulled" several cribeful of ill-smelling, but decidedly material, human being s who were sent up for vagrancy and petty theft.

—*The Galveston Daily News*
May 4, 1885

❖ ❖ ❖

The Ghost Of Grand Prairie
How The Good People Were Rattled By An Opossum

GRAND PRAIRIE- The little and the great are linked together in this life and a great many believe that the present is linked to the future. Such was the opinion that prevailed in the community of Grand

Prairie last week on the report gaining currency that a ghost from the land of the hereafter was materializing in the residence of Mr. Robert Merryman. Lake Virgil's story, the report gained strength as it traveled and by the time it had reached the margin of the woods that skirt the prairie the spook of Caesar in the tent of Brutus was a mere shiver compared with the congestive chills that, like ice water, ran down the spines of the good religious people in that highly respected community. They had several ghosts mixed up and of all manner of shapes, and behavior, from an angel of peace bending downward from the sky, like a rainbow in a creaking silk dress and bangs, to a boisterous demon with gleaming eyes, delighting in smashing kettles and pans and painting the business red generally. A force of investigators —county family reporters—finally took up the affair and boiled it down to the facts that dishes were rattled and somebody thought he had observed a shadow passing before his eyes. In this there was at least the shadow of a ghost. There was nothing like the Rochester knockings; nothing like the siege laid to a horse in Brownsville a few years ago when a whole brickyard was used for ammunition, and nothing like the lone man who haunted the capital at Austin and probably plugged up the chimney in the Attorney General's office to the final destruction of the building by fire.

The citizens of the prairie, as they heard the latest version of the affair, began to rest easier and the babies to talk less about rawhead and bloody bones. And now comes the finale. It appears that on Monday night the manifestations were stronger than usual, and Mr. Merryman, who is a man of strong courage, resolved, in the language of the poet, to "the mystery explore." Accordingly he struck a light and loaded himself with a clear conscience, without which no person is fit to salute a visitor from the other world. Thus armed he proceeded to explore, looking up at the ceiling and in through the keyhole and down at the floor. The last look made the whole thing clear as the noonday sun, and there were no "angels and ministers of grace defend is about it." It was nothing but a 'possum playing ghost, and Mr. Merryman brought the séance to a close with a club.

—*Dallas Morning News*
November 5, 1885

❖ ❖ ❖

A Ghost Loose In Stringtown

STRINGTOWN- The colored people of Springtown are agitated over what they term the visitations of the ghost of a deceased voodoo priest. It first materialized last Thursday night, and manifested itself in a hostile assault with bricks and stones on the residence of Mack Darnell, driving his dogs and his children under the bed. Mack seized his old Queen Ann and shot at a tall, white figure which then disappeared with a sizzling noise. Since that occurrence the ghost has been besieging houses nightly, despite the Constitution of the United States and the amendments thereto.

—*Dallas Morning News*
February 16, 1886

A Kuklux Ghost

STRINGTOWN- The colored sovereigns of Stringtown are much exercised over what they describe as a wild white man with a shotgun, who, for several successive nights, has been seen crawling along their street as if he was expecting to flush plovers. They say that he is not the ghost about which so much has been told because they can tell that ghost by his hair.
—*Dallas Morning News*
March 19, 1886

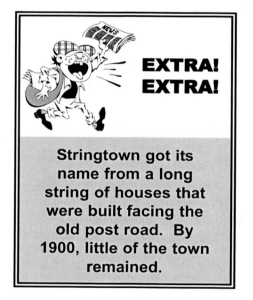

Stringtown got its name from a long string of houses that were built facing the old post road. By 1900, little of the town remained.

Ghostly Indignation
Sheol Breaks Loose
In The Third Ward

SAN ANTONIO- Third Ward darkies have been very much excited for the past three or four days over a haunted house in the vicinity of Chestnut Street. It is alleged that the ghosts or supernatural visitors are in the habit of throwing stones and brick-bats in at the windows at all hours of the night, endangering the live of the occupants. The particular object of the ghostly indignation seems to be in the person of the small boy occupant, he having been banged up by the rocks more than the others. No one as yet has been able to see where the missiles come from or who throws them, and in consequence the excitement among the colored folks has become intense. The only explanation attempted is that the little boy has found some money that does not belong to him, and has made no effort to return it to the lawful owner: hence the effort to compel him to do so by spirits.

If all the evil doers in San Antonio were subjected to a like ordeal, such a pandemonium would reign that the community would be convinced that Sheol had broken loose indeed.
—*San Antonio Daily Express*
August 10, 1886

Sheol is the abode of the dead, the under-world. The place of departed spirits (Hades).

CHAPTER 2 GHOSTS

The Supernatural
A Thrilling Ghost Story From
The Second Ward

DALLAS- From the days of Cicero, who related the thrilling case of the two youth of Megara, and in fact behind Cicero's days, stretching away back toward the dawn of the creation, ghost stories have been handed down through the mists of time, and have served, if no other purpose, the useful one of helping to keep history spiced and otherwise embalmed. Virgil would have proved a shapeless wreck on the strand of the middle ages, without its ghost story, and no first-class old play—as Hamlet, for instance—could prosper without one.

In modern times, too, a rising city can no more afford to be without its ghost than a jaybird can fly without a tail. Kansas City has had several, and now Dallas wheels into line with a regular teeth-shatterer, forty degrees below zero. The scene is laid in Second Ward—that ward which stood rock-ribbed for the man of its choice in the late congressional campaign—and the circumstances as related to a News reporter yesterday are as follows: For some time back a good Christian family, who have an aversion to seeing their names in print, have heard unaccountable noises in their house at night, which recently have taken on more decided manifestations, as if a case of the jim-jams which escaped from its owner found the latch-string on the outside and had come to stay. In the latter stage furniture would be rudely thrown around, and on more than one occasion the hands of the family would feel hands passed over their faces with—G.

Whilliken—all the clammy feeling of death. The man of the house informed the neighbors and some of them kept watch, but they did not seem to be on rapport with the ghostly visitors and they watched in vain. Last Monday night the climax of terror was reached, when at the dreary hour when churchyards yawn the same cold clammy hands were passed over the faces of the presiding family elders and the next moment found the bed in which the aforesaid elders lay whirling across the floor. The parties thus rudely treated by the unseen jumped out of bed, suffering from congestion and spent the remainder of the night in terror and prayer with the full blaze of a lamp beaming on their pallid countenances.

The gentleman who relates this experience says it is not all, some of the antics of the phantom being too queer for recital. The family moved out of the neighborhood yesterday, but the Second Ward, which is being prominently brought to the surface by the strange event, proposes to explore the mystery, and an opportunity is offered to young men of an inquiring turn of mind to test their nerves. Some of the people of the neighborhood attributive the affair to a combination of imagination or that an army of rates trained to hauling freight could not well move a bed and its two human occupants.

When such things are related by parties with no object for deception, who must be aware that the tendency of public thought is to ridicule the supernatural and whose statements tally as to facts, it is claimed by the thinking people whom *The News* reporter saw yesterday that the subject is a fit one for investigation. It is amusing to hear the matter discussed on the streets. One young man last evening expressed a willingness to set up all night in the sanctuary of spiritual visitation, but his neighbor—also a young man—declined an invitation to be his companion, and said that the performance of such a duty should be undertaken by the police. Another gentleman suggested that as nerve will be needed in the new government it might be well to have the candidates take turn about in waiting on the ghost.

—*Dallas Morning News*
March 9, 1887

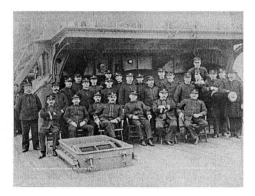

The Phantom Excitement
Drawing A Stream Of Visitors.
What A News Reporter Learned.
Pistol Shots. Groans.
A Woman In White.
Flight Of The Cook.

DALLAS- Dr. Arch Cochran and Mr. William Greenlaw spent Tuesday night in the reported haunted house on Griffin Street, but either the ghost did not care to entertain such distinguished guests, or it may have been its off night, as it came not.

Both of the gentlemen, through the night long, kept their eyes strained and their ears cocked for specters, but neither heard nor saw anything that could not be accounted for through the operation of natural laws.

A News reporter, guided by the light of the bright Polar star, visited the scene of the spiritual disturbances last night and found quite a stream of people engaged in a like mission. There were white people and black people, but while the former knocked at the door and asked for the latest developments, the latter clung to the distant fences like "coons" and were satisfied with what the returning visitors would tell them, which was frequently highly exaggerated. The reporter met a young lady, a member of the family, who said that the stream of visitors had been unbroken since morning. She had made up her mind not to remain another night in the house, and she had only remained there that long because her mother had been sick as the result of the shock which her nerves underwent at the hands of the apparition, whose antics threw the Rochester knockings entirely in the shade.

The family, to follow up the recital of the young lady, which was given on condition that her name should not appear in print, moved into the house about a month ago. A few nights later the young lady's parents were aroused by what they imagined was somebody trying to pull the blankets off the bed, speedily followed by a movement of the bed itself, which was rudely twisted and shaken by what on examination proved to be unseen hands. These manifestations were followed or accompanied on different nights by others of a still more blood-curdling character. Pistol shots would be heard seemingly fired in the hall and followed by smothered groans like those of a woman or a child, which at times would be accompanied by voices too indistinct to catch their meaning. The shots were distinctly heard by Mr. Greenlaw and other neighbors, who imagined that they must have been fired at dogs or for other purposed not inconsistent with earthly existence.

It is also affirmed that the ghost materialized to an old lady, approaching her with the soft movement of a moonbeam, and appearing as a white woman in a white garment. The apparition placed over the old lady's face its hands which felt like the puff of a cold damp norther. The old lady muttered, "What do you want?" and the apparition vanished into thin air at the sound of the question. At times, with the full light turned on, sounds are heard as if produced by a rubber ball bouncing on the floor and striking at short intervals and distances.

The window curtains have been rattled and the windows knocked on as if with knuckles, while the shining moon disclosed no presence. The colored cook, as might be expected, did not stand it alone. Early in the proceedings, as she was engaged at the work of preparing supper, her dress was pulled violently. Turning around, with the exclamation "Fore God! What dat!" she discovered nothing. Her next movement was homeward bound and she had not since returned. It would be begging the question, in face of the evidence of the senses, to say that there is nothing in all this, and the case presents an opportunity

for the local mediums to establish their reputation by an exploration of the mystery. *The News* reporter was informed that there are no rats in the house, and that some of the manifestations have been witnessed by strong lamplight.

—*Dallas Morning News*
March 10, 1887

❖ ❖ ❖

Haunted House

DALLAS- Crowds gather to visit the haunted house on Griffin Street. A News reporter interviewed the family who moved out to-day, and was told of blood-curdling manifestations, pistol shots, followed by groans, are heard, and the apparition of a white woman robed in white has been seen by an old lady, a strict church member. Dr. Arch. Cochran, the late Republican candidate for governor of Texas, sat up last night but saw nothing. Policemen are performing a like duty to-night.

—*Galveston Daily News*
March 11, 1887

❖ ❖ ❖

The Ghost

DALLAS- The Griffin Street ghost has lost its grip as a sensation. Since the family fled in terror from the house, there has been no one to report the acts of the shadow, and the people have turned their attention to more substantial things. A ghost, like a business firm must keep before the public—must advertise or be advertised—

or the public will soon forget it, and if the Griffin Street ghost wants to continue it must give some sign or token that it is still doing business at the old stand, or that it has opened out in more centrally located quarters.

—*Dallas Morning News*
March 14, 1887

A Veritable Ghost
Dallas Boasts Of Having The Only First-class Sensation In The State. A Tailor Badly Scared Up.

DALLAS- The Griffin Street ghost which about three months ago forced a deputy United States marshal to evacuate his premises, has turned up again, the besieged this time being the family of W.P. Meeks, a tailor who did not believe in ghosts and undertook to inhabit the haunted house.

Meeks to-day acknowledged that the phenomena had become intolerable and that he and Mrs. Malcomsin's family, who occupy one-half of the house will move out to-morrow. They hear groans, see a white object floating in the air and observe

the furniture moved rudely. Last night the bed occupied by Miss Meeks was raised in the air, and she, after jumping out ran screaming to her father's room. Dogs will not stay in the house at night. The existence of the phantom is now corroborated by upward of a score of witnesses, some of whom are known to have no faith in the supernatural, and are considered credible witnesses.

—*The Galveston Daily News*
June 11, 1887

❖ ❖ ❖

The Ghost

DALLAS- The Griffin Street ghost is reported to be again on deck. Mr. William F. Meek, who assisted on bearding the phantom in its den, informed a News reporter yesterday that the racket was becoming intolerable, and that he and other occupants of the house would move out to-day.

—*Dallas Morning News*
June 11, 1887

❖ ❖ ❖

Spooks At Whitewright
They Gave White Beards And Glaring Eyes, Ghastly Careworn Faces.

WHITEWRIGHT- The ghosts mentioned in Sunday's News continue to appear in the house in the southern portion of the city. Last night P.O. Clemmons and a friend concluded they would go down to the haunted house and make the spooks a visit.

When Mr. Clemmons and friend arrived at the house everything was quiet, but they were not there long before one of the specters made its appearance at one of the windows in the building. They describe the apparition as having long white bead, fiery red eyes and a ghastly pale face, with a careworn look.

They demanded of the ghostship what its business was there, but receiving no answer they threw rocks at the specter and it disappeared in the darkness. The ghost story has been going the rounds here for some time. But this is the only instance in which anybody has ever ventured out to investigate. It is the opinion of a great many people that some wag had dressed himself up in a ghostly manner to have fun out of the superstitious, while the believers of spooks say it was a genuine ghost. There are colored people in town who will not go near the house at night for love or money. A crowd of boys has agreed to go out and see what it is, and if it is a joke some man is playing he may get the worst of it.

—*Dallas Morning News*
January 10, 1888

❖ ❖ ❖

Spooks

WHITEWRIGHT- Apparitions continue to appear in the haunted house. As yet no one had ventured on the home at night to make a thorough investigation.

—*Dallas Morning News*
March 30, 1888

His Spirit Returns To Jail
Conrad Jackson's Ghost Appears In The Cell Occupied By Him Before His Execution.
Waco Making The Anvils Thunder Forth Her Rejoicings.

WACO- Morris Richey, an intelligent colored man who is in the county jail awaiting action on his appeal, say Conrad Jackson's ghost entered the cell he lately in life occupied and sat on his hammock at midnight after he was hung.

—*Dallas Morning News*
July 18, 1888

❖ ❖ ❖

A Haunted House

SHERMAN- There is a haunted house on North Travis Street where at 8:10 each evening a report similar to the discharge of a shot can be heard by those on the inside of the house but cannot be heard by one on the outside.

—*Dallas Morning News*
January 19, 1889

❖ ❖ ❖

A Talkative Ghost

COMMERCE- It is said that a dwelling on Seventh Street, near Commerce, is haunted with ghosts or spirit rappers. When there is a light in the house all is quiet, but the moment it is extinguished the parings begin, and the ghostship, by means

of raps will even answer questions asked. The manifestation has excited considerable stir and much comment.

—*Dallas Morning News*
October 25, 1889

❖ ❖ ❖

Ghost Of Wolfe Trail

**An Indian Ghost Said To Have Been Seen By A Milkman.
Bob Chapman, The Nurse, Relates Some Of His Experiences With Dallas Ghosts.
How Three Shadows Caught Him By The Legs.
A Headless Man.**

DALLAS- "Did you hear about the ghost on Wolfe Trail?" was the question addressed by Mr. J. Juniger to a News reporter yesterday.

"No, what is it?"

"Well, they say that parties have seen a ghost dance there lately. I know nothing about it of my own knowledge. I guess there are some Indians up there selling arrows and it is an easy matter to make up a ghost dance when Indians are around."

Capt., W.H. Lemnon, who lives near Wolfe Trail, said there were no Indians in that neighborhood and he knew nothing of the ghost dance.

He added, "Go ahead and investigate it."

"I have heard people talking about an Indian having been seen dancing over an old grave near Wolfe Trail," said Capt. Joe Record.

"They say that an Indian chief was buried there long, long ago, and that he was seen dancing around his grave during the troubles in Dakota."

The appearance of a ghost was a common report, but the best that cold be learned about it was that a milkman while going home late at night a few weeks ago saw an Indian with a great tail feather in the back of his head, long, black hair and a coat of war paint on his face. The Indian eyed him closely, and his team would not move until the savage disappeared. The Indian did not dance and neither did he sing.

While investigating the weird rumor the reporter came across Bob Chapman, a colored nurse, who is known as a ghost expert, and is reputed to have more of the summer lad folks around him than a necromancer.

"Do you know anything about that ghost, Bob?"

"Which ghost, sah?"

"The ghost of Wolfe Trail."

"Ise heard something 'bout it: I thought you was quirin bout the ghost that I saw on the Central railroad."

"What about that ghost?"

"Well, hates to talk about such things."

"Oh, go on, Bob."

"Well, a few months ago one bright night, as I was walking along the midnight I sees near where the road crosses Ross Avenue a pet colt standing on the track. As I came up to the colt I looked under his belly and there on the other side of him stood a man without a head. I fell over 'ginst the colt and fainted. As I fell the colt felt like a ball of cotton. Unless my mind is all 'magination there are ghosts and I sees or hears 'em all the time."

What The Door Said

"I was cleaning Mr. Smith's room the other day and had shet the door, a great big heavy door, and was dusting off the mirror, when all at once the door said: 'Click up,' and flew wide open. I said, 'Come in, sah,' but there was nobody thar: so I shet it tight and saw that the bolt turned. Then I goes to dusting again and a minute or so later—it mightn't be so long, for I wanted to get away and the minutes seemed to be a mile long—the door again said 'click up' and opened. There was nobody there, I'll swear to that. Well that nearly knocked me, but I shet the door again and walked back to the bureau with the dust-brush in my hand and listened. 'Click up' says the door a third time and flew open. I says, 'come in, come in,' and I grabs my hat and runs downstairs. I jest flew and I tole Mr. Smith there was a haunt upstairs."

Electric Light Ghosts

"The worsest ghost I ever saw in my life was a few nights ago on Main Street. You knew Mr. --------, the white gentleman who died here?"

"Yes, Bob know him very well."

"Don't mention his name. I see him very often and he looks zactly as he did in life. He smiles every time we meet jes as in life and I'd jedge he's as happy on the other side of Jorden as when he was here. Well. He does not scare me a bit, and I was thinking of him going up Main Street when I saw-----I saw--------I saw I was followed by three shadows. There was a shadow on one side of me and two were behind me."

"Oh, nonsense, Bob; those shadows were caused by three 5000-candle power electric lights shinning on you from different directions."

"No, sir; there was no electrical light 'bout it. They was shadows. I crooked up my leg and the shadows crooked up and then I knowed that they had me by the legs. I ran away up the street and near the post office I turns round and I only saw one shadow. That's a haunt, says I, for shu, and the goose flesh broke out all over me and my hair stood up like the feathers on a frizzled hen."

A Blood Congealer

"I nursed a man here one time and he died. His name was—well, I declare, I forgot it. But anyway he was a stranger, and he had no relatives. The night 'fore he died he says to me: 'Bob, look at all them dogs; drive them away.' It looked a kind of curious to me, for the man did not drink, and so I says, 'There is no dogs here.' "

"Oh, yes there is," he answered. "Look at that big black dog sitting on the foot of the

bed. Drive him away, Bob; drive him away."

"The man died that night and as he was dying the two lamps I had in the room commenced going down. I picked up the lamps and shook them. It was no good. They burned down lower and lower and they went out altogether jes as the man died. I ran down stairs to the telephone and I rang up the place where the corpse used to work, when suddenly without any noise a man came down behind me, and says: 'He's dead.' I looked at the man and he disappeared right in my presence. It was the ghost of the dead man. Then my hair riz, I felt a heavy weight press on me, and I would not go back to the room. I went to the party for whom the corpse worked and had it taken to the undertakers. Ask Mr. ----- if that's not so. He is the man who looked after the corpse."

—Dallas Morning News
January 23, 1891

❖ ❖ ❖

A Haunted House
Voice Of The Flying Day

DALLAS- "I have just heard of a haunted house which I am going to watch carefully," says Walter Besant. He adds that "it has been standing vacant for some time, but was recently taken by a family. They began by complaining that they could not sleep at night. Noises were heard; they seemed like footsteps; a cold breath in their faces started them into wakefulness. The father of the family said it was all nonsense; he would not hear of such rubbish;

the family should put such things out of their minds. They prepared, therefore, to bear their sufferings and their terrors with a Spartan attitude. Meantime the nervous condition of the girls became almost intolerable, and I know not what would have happened had not the father himself one morning on coming down to breakfast made an announcement. 'We are going to leave this house to-day,' he said, banging the table with his fist, 'this very day.' In an hour or two the vans came round and the furniture went to temporary lodgings. I am curious to learn what will happen when the next family moves in. And I am most anxious to find out what the old man saw."

—Dallas Morning News
December 28, 1891

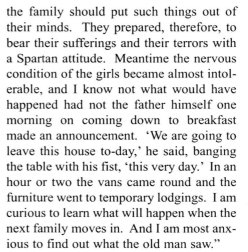

Startling Apparitions
Robed In Snowy White Called Up In
A Spiritualistic Séance.
They Walked Out
In Front Of The Audience.
A Spirit Woman Kisses Her Babe.

DALLAS- Prof. H. Pettibone gave a materializing séance last night at the Watkins Hotel on Swiss Avenue, in the presence of twenty-eight persons. At the request of Prof. Pettibone a committee was selected from the audience to make a careful inspection of the medium, the rooms and the cabinet, which was done. There was nothing in the cabinet but a common chair. The medium then went into the cabinet and sat down dropping the curtains in front of him. The audience gently sang a hymn and before it was concluded the curtains parted and a child about four feet high appeared in the center. It was arrayed in a loose flowing garment of pure white. The lamp in the rear of the room gave sufficient light for all to see the forms of the apparitions and those who were near the cabinet could distinguish the faces. The second form to appear was said to be a spirit lady, height about 5 foot 4 inches. She was dressed in white. She waved her hand toward Mrs. J.M. Hurd and nodded her head as if she was her sister, Emma Palmer.

Next came two white forms at once, one in the center between the two front curtains and the other at the corner. They did not get entirely out in plain view as the others did. Next appeared a long white bare arm and hand through the top of the cabinet, reaching nearly eight feet high. Then a lady in white appeared. She was some-what taller then the former female figure and the audience was singing, so the name was not heard.

Then came a little boy about three feet tall, and next appeared a lady who stated to be Sarah, the mother of a Dallas gentleman. He stated that Mr. or Mrs. Pettibone had never heard anything about his mother or her name. Mrs. Hurd then asked her sister to come again and she appeared with her baby, who died about the time she did. This spirit was like the others, dressed in white and was plainly visible to all. She fondled the baby in her arms and bent down and kissed it.

Then there appeared a form of a tall, slender lady whose name was not given and immediately following her appearance came a little girl 10 to 12 years old apparently, with a little bundle in her arms which looked like a doll. She kissed it several times just as any little girl would kiss her doll-baby. Her name was given as Susie Baldwin and her sister is said to be in Galveston.

Soon after she vanished there appeared a tall apparition with a white turban on the head, wearing a long black beard and shrouded in a long cloak. This was stated to be an Egyptian spirit, one of Prof. Pettibone's guests. The next to appear was a man spirit, whose name was given as Hail Reed from Pennsylvania. This was followed by a beautiful female form, giving the name of Mrs. Pettus. Soon after she retired a dark faced apparition with long straight black hair stood between the curtains. This was said to be Redman, an Indian guide, whose disappearance was followed by a lace and shoulders, stated to be a brother of Mrs. J.C. Watkins.

The next most remarkable exhibition was the appearance of a lovely young lady robed in a white dress. She stepped out far enough to take a rose from a lady in the audience. This was stated to be the spirit of Genie Watkins. Next appeared a man with black beard, stated to be a brother of Capt. Watkins. Another white form followed but no name was given.

Then there was quite a pause and the controlling spirit stated that it was so warm in the cabinet that the medium should be brought out at once. When the curtain was raised Prof. Pettibone was lying back in the chair unconscious and trembling like a leaf. Fanning and rubbing his temples soon brought him out all right. The first thing he said was: "I'm all right now. Where is the committee?" The committee made another examination and reported nothing but the chair in the cabinet, and where those forms came from and how the white clothing became so plainly visible to all was a mystery to many in the audience.

—*Dallas Morning News*
July 20, 1892

The Dead Do Walk

DALLAS- The Fifth Ward neighborhood has been troubled for some time past by the nocturnal visits of a supposed spirit from the world beyond. The ghost is usually seen in the early morning, between 2 and 4 o'clock and its visits are almost immediately after "pay day." Every ghost has its own peculiarities. This one's is to blow out the electric lights. It is all done in a moment. The vision will emerge from some alleyway and stride at once to the electric pole, and with a majestic wave of its skeleton arm extinguish the light and disappear in the dark. The colored people in the neighborhood, and no small portion of the white people, are beginning to have a sort of scared expression on their faces each night as the shades begin to fall.

—*Dallas Morning News*
August 26, 1892

❖ ❖ ❖

A Strange Vision
The citizens Of Callisburg Are Greatly Torn Up

GAINESVILLE- The people living in the Callisburg community, twelve miles east of Gainesville, are greatly torn up over a strange vision that appears nightly on the old Si Farris place, three miles east of Callisburg. It appears at times in the shape of a large ball of fire and again is in the shape of an illuminated man. Hundreds of people have seen it on different occasions. Quite a number of the best citizens of the community, who are in town to-day, vouch for the statement that it is there.

Among those who are here to-day are Green Norman, E. Phelps and Gaston Hawkins, and they gave *The News* man a graphic description of the phenomenon. They say it sometimes appears as a bright light, sometimes it is blue, again it is blood red and then it will appear in all these colors at once. Just before the light appears a noise resembling that of a person failing heavily upon the floor is heard about the house. Hundreds of people are flocking there nightly to see it. Last Saturday night there were nearly 200 people on the ground at one time, some of whom had come all the way from Grayson country. Quite a number have chased the thing on horseback, but it flees when anyone approaches.

It was first seen one night during last December by a young man while sitting up with the corpse of a man named Bidwell who had suicided by shooting himself in the head. He saw it then in the shape of a man and it was not seen again until a few weeks ago, and since it has appeared almost nightly. It is a mystery and one that is puzzling the heads of a large number of serious people.

—*Dallas Morning News*
October 4, 1892

❖ ❖ ❖

Haunted Schoolhouse
Hawk Eye's Experience With An Eolian Spook Fiddle

VAN ALSTYNE- A young writing master form Denison commenced a writing class at Hawk Eye schoolhouse, near here. A crowd of boys of the neighborhood conceived the idea of having some fun at the expense of the young professor. They procured a spool of thread and unwinding what they needed attached one end to a nail under the caves of the roof, then getting sufficient distance from the house to avoid detection began rubbing the string vigorously with a piece of rosin. It had the desired effect, A general stampede ensued among the scholars, during which they tumbled over each other promiscuously in trying to make their exit from the haunted building. The young professor drew his pistol and fired three shots through the roof and ran from the house yelling and firing his pistol at every step. As the result of having a little fun the boys were arrested for malicious mischief, while the professor is charged with carrying pistol. They will have their trials here Saturday.

—*Dallas Morning News*
April 20, 1893

HIDDEN HEADLINES of TEXAS

Ghosts In The Alamo
The Old Superstition
Finds Some New Converts.
Mysterious Sounds
In The Old Historic Building
Reported By The Police.
Don't Like The Place.

SAN ANTONIO- There is a legend among the Mexicans that when it rains and the wind howls wildly around the old Alamo building, where in 1836 so many brave and patriotic Texans were butchered by Santa Anna's soldiers, the ghosts of the departed heroes or some of them, notably those of Davy Crockett, Bowie and Travis, arise and stalk about the old building with the measured tread of heavily armed and booted men on guard. These old stories have been heard for years, but nobody except the Mexicans have ever believed that there was anything but superstition in them, but since the old building has been dignified, or undignified by the use of the small new part on the side, which has been built in since the famous fight, as a police station some startling statements have been made with regard to the ghostly per-ambulations of the shades of the heroes if it is the shades of those gentlemen which are responsible for the alleged goings on.

Certainly if there is a spot in earth where it might be expected that the earth so reeks with noble blood as to cause the people to expect that the ghosts of the dead walk uneasy there, it is the Alamo in San Antonio.

That part of the building where the police station is located is on the side of the low space with a window where the Mexicans finally broke in and slaughtered the defenders. The window is not very big, but had double iron bars and the wall is perhaps five feet thick through which it is cut. This opens directly from that room where the two mounted officers who are detailed at the station sit. Adjoining this room is a small cell room which has been used for some time, and since the police station has been opened stories have been circulated to the effect that some prisoners who were confined there at various times had complained of strange noises in the main building, and always on dark rainy nights. They heard walking and the rat-tling of muskets and chains.

The two policemen, who are as brave as policemen usually are, also insist that they had heard very strange sounds in the main building and always on dark, rainy nights. Officer Froboese stated to a reporter for the Express the other night that soon after the station was opened and when the recent hard rains began he was standing near the door alone one night when he thought he heard someone walking heavily inside the main building. He went and looked through the grating and asked who was there, but it was too dark to see. There was no reply, but the heavy tramp of the boots continued for some time. He said that he had heard the sound often during the rains, but when the rain stopped the sounds were heard no more. The policeman said he was not afraid, but he was positive about the noise, although he made no pretense at explaining it and didn't know whether it was ghosts or not.

Besides Officer Froboese, other officers state that they have heard the sounds, but

none of them ever saw anything. Officer Froboese said that he thought perhaps they could see "something" if they should put out the lights and sit in the dark a while on a stormy night. He invited the reporter for the Express to visit the station on a rainy night and listen to the sounds, but rainy nights are not that frequent in San Antonio at this season of the year and it may be some time before another opportunity occurs.

The interior of the old building is in a badly dilapidated condition. The upper room is separated from the lower one by a rough floor, and there are numerous wooden posts supporting it. The floor of the lower room consists of loose boards laid on light sills, which rattle when one walks over them. There being nothing at all in the building the echo was loud, and it was suggested by the reporter that rats or a cat or some other animal might be responsible for the noise, but the officers say that it is impossible that it should be a cat or any other animal.

When the reporter was sitting in the station at 10 o'clock in the forenoon the other day he heard the sound of the feet of someone walking back and forth in the interior. It was the boy who has charge of the place, but as the youth isn't there at night the disturbance can not be charged to him. The big officer who patrols the Alamo plaza said to the reporter that he had often heard the story.

"Do you believe the sounds are heard?" asked the reporter.

"O, yes; there's no doubt about it."

"How do you account for them?"

"Well, it's only the ignorant Mexicans who believe it is ghost. Perhaps it is rats," said the officer. "It is a fact that negro prisoners say they have heard people walking and chains rattling all night," he continued, "and it is almost impossible to get negroes into the cell. Some people say that they would as soon sleep in the Alamo as not, but I wouldn't do it for anything."

" I suppose it is because the rats might bite you," suggested the reporter.

"It's all right about the rats," he replied, "there's been too many men killed in there for a man to feel comfortable in the place. I am not afraid of ghosts. I don't believe in them, but I tell you I wouldn't sleep in there."

The custodian when asked stated that he didn't know anything about the ghosts in the place. He had not seen any apparition arise from the corner where Davy Crockett fell beside a pile of Mexican dead nor heard anything to indicate that the shade of Bowie was hovering around the little cell room in the interior where he was butchered while lying sick. But the custodian is only around in the day time and you know ghosts don't get out of their place of seclusion and do military duty in the day time.

Now the reader may wonder why the noises are supposed to occur on rainy nights, but if he has read faithfully, as every good Texan has, the story of the Alamo he will remember that at the time of the capture by the Mexican butchers it was stormy weath-

er, so that aside from the general theory that ghosts walk on dark and stormy nights there is ample reason why in this particular case the sighting of the wind and the dash of rain against the old walls should cause them to get to feeling uncomfortable and go on military duty against the besieging greasers again.

A gentleman who lived for some time in the house adjoining the Alamo says he never heard any ghosts walk except at the office where he works, but he admits that his digestion and conscience are both quite good and that he never staid awake listening on dark and stormy nights or ventured into the historic pile of stones and mortar after dark, so that counts for nothing. People have heard the ghosts and nobody has come forward to prove that it was rats or dripping water or the workings of the imagination.

—*Dallas Morning News*
June 11, 1893

Each year dozens of strange and mysterious happenings are still reported to occur at the Alamo.

A Haunted House

PALESTINE- The negroes in the eastern part of Old Town are considerably excited over a house that they claim to be haunted. A negro woman was making up a bed a few mornings ago and as soon as she would get the covering straightened out it would fly back. The operation was repeated several times and the woman flew to a neighboring cabin screaming at the top of her voice. Other negroes went over and tried to make up the bed but each time the bedding would become disturbed. The negroes are worked up over the affair.

—*Dallas Morning News*
April 9, 1894

Ghost Of The Brazos

WACO- The people settled on the shores of the Brazos River above Waco are puzzled with reports told by boatman and fisherman to the effect that a corpse is seen occasionally on the surface spinning in eddies and moving in eccentric lines in the water. Various persons, white and black declare they have seen the floater appear and disappear as if he arose to the surface to look around after which he dives and goes out of sight. Two boys who went past the mouth of the Bosque in a boat say they saw the body plainly and made out from the face, which was somewhat disfigured by nibbling fish, that it is the remains of a young white man. Justice Bayless Earle sent a deputy constable to-day to investigate the mystery of the dead man, which some declare has the power to float up stream, and keeps hanging around near where the Bosque joins the Brazos.

—*Dallas Morning News*
May 2, 1896

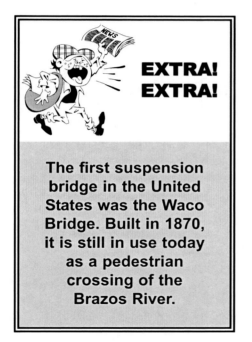

EXTRA! EXTRA!

The first suspension bridge in the United States was the Waco Bridge. Built in 1870, it is still in use today as a pedestrian crossing of the Brazos River.

A Ghost On A Bike

WACO- Tom Carter, a colored man, who lives near the Falls County line, tells a strange story of seeing a ghost on a bicycle. "I was on my way to Waco last night," Tom said, "and just before the moon rose I stopped to light a cigarette. The wind blew my match out and as I did not have another I was about to give up my smoke. Just then a man on a wheel rode up with a cigar in his mouth. My pony was frightened, but I held him tight and asked the gentleman for a light. He was silent, but just as polite as could be, and he let me get a light from his cigar. I struck a trot, and the wheelman kept the middle of the road ahead of me. My pony kept snorting and trembling and now and then the lantern on the bicycle made a strong blue light, which terrified poultry in the yards we passed and set hens to cackling and ducks to quacking. I tried to keep my eyes on the figure ahead of me, but man and wheel would fade out and come again. All of a sudden the wheelman and his wheel disappeared and after that my pony went along easy. I am sure it was a spirit. My mouth is sore from smoking the cigarette he lit for me from fire on his cigar."

—*Dallas Morning News*
November 28, 1896

❖ ❖ ❖

Haunted House Torn Down

SAN ANTONIO- The old haunted house on the San Jun Road near Riverside Park, has been torn down and only the debris of the old adobe walls now mark the spot.

—*San Antonio Daily Light*
December 13, 1896

Borders On The Miraculous

PARIS- A mystery is reported from Seven Mile Creek, this county, that borders well nigh in to the miraculous. The facts in the case are these: One John Blassingame moved to the vicinity named a few weeks since from Polk County, Arkansas, and leased a portion of what is know as the Yates farm. He was accompanied by his family. Shortly after their arrival his wife was taken seriously ill with what proved to the dreaded typhoid pneumonia. The poor woman had been ill but a few days when she became insane and raved incessantly, finally dying two nights ago. Here is where the mystery begun. A few moments after her death a dim white spot was noticed to appear on one of the side rails of the bedstead upon which the corpse was yet lying. The mysterious spot first appeared near the foot of the bedstead and gradually became larger, when suddenly it commenced to change into a strange form. This evolution was kept up until the figure of a white rabbit was outlined as perfectly as perfect could be.

The bedstead was highly cherished and comparatively new. This strange phenomena, if phenomena it can be called, was witnessed by fully a dozen persons who sat up with the corpse and scores of others who have called at the residence since. The figure of the rabbit is yet plainly visible upon the bedstead; in fact, it is plainer than when it first appeared. No amount of friction seems to have any effect upon I whatever. The occurrence has created nothing less than a sensation in the neighborhood and it is regarded as a miracle by the superstitious.

—*Dallas Morning News*
December 13, 1896

The Floating Ghost
The True Story Of A Haunt Seen By A Texas Boy

PITTSBURG- Bert closed his father's store one dark misty night in January to go home. As he left the lighted streets he muttered to himself, a la Gov. Hogg (for he had just heard that expression used by the eloquent governor), "By gatlins; it is dark as pitch, and I've got to walk half a mile and no lantern."

But as he knew the road well he trudged bravely off, whistling to himself for company. Now, Bert had been nursed, as most southern children are by a good old negress called a "black mammy." And she, in order to inculcate obedience in his childhood, had initiated him into all the occult mystery of voudoism, "haunts," hobgoblins etc. Bert firmly believed it was the gospel truth then, cause black mammy said so. When he grew naughty and disobedient she had only to say "I'll make dem haunts ketch you chile," and he grew very humble and obedient all at once.

But as he grew older and got out from under her tutelage and his mind grew more broad and cultured he looked upon his old black mammy's tales in their proper light, and, so he thought, relegated them into the shades of oblivion. Bert was now a tall, well-built and courageous lad of 17. tonight as he stumbled along through the misty gloom he thought of the old vacant and dilapidated house that he was nearing on his way home, which the superstitious folk in the vicinity said was haunted sure. But as Burt had passed it often and had never seen anything more spooky than a few "weary Willies," or tramps, occasionally, he long since conceded that story to be mere bosh.

But now he seemed to have a presentiment of a coming danger, for he fancied he heard strange noises in the air around him, and now as the old house loomed up close by he actually began to grow frightened. Realizing that this was all foolishness he soliloquized thusly to himself, "Bert you're no fool: you know better than to get scared at an old empty house like a would-be voudoued negro. Come brace up! Be somebody." And it was well that he did "brace," for at this auspicious moment he heard an unearthly groan and at the same instant saw a white form arise directly in front of him until it was fully four feet high. Seemingly it floated in the air, for he could see nothing to hold it up.

Now I have said Bert was a courageous lad, but it took his courage to face that thing, which kept moving slowly along in front of him. He thought of old back mammy and her weird tales and wondered if it were possible that at last he was destined to see a real, genuine ghost, and that at any rate, here was something that he would always swear was one, unless he found out otherwise. But how was he to find out? He was by himself. He had no arms of any kind. Most any one would have felt braver with a weapon of some sort. Besides, he had not lost this particular ghost, and did not care to attack it alone and singlehanded. He would have been only too glad to have passed and gone on home unsatisfied as to what kind of ghost it was.

As the lane here was very narrow and this demon shade still kept floating along ahead of him in awful silence he could not pass it without coming in contact with it. If he went around, the fields were muddy and he certainly would be laughed at, for he had often boasted that if he ever saw a spook he was going to see what it was or die. He realized this was the longed-for opportunity. It was now or never. And he bravely determined to bring things to a focus, to run at it, scare it, catch it, or at least run through it, and get on the side next to home, upon which even if the spook chased him he thought grimly that the race of Tam-o-Shanter wouldn't be in it at all.

So suiting his actions to the thought he sprang at the spook with a quick bound, and to his immense astonishment he had grabbed a tough scrawny something that

was evidently was very much alive, and not spooked by any means. For when he jumped back in shocked surprise it hit him with a resounding whack across the shins that reminded him very forcibly of the rush and kick of a certain member of a rival football team he had played with not long since.

All at once it dawned upon him that the kick came from a live and evidently very healthy white 2-year-old calf with black legs and feet, which in the darkness and wet he could neither see nor hear. His heart gradually resumed its normal operations and laughing heartily at his fertile imagination he went on his way a hardened and permanent skeptic of mysticism.

—*Dallas Morning News*
August 1, 1897

❖ ❖ ❖

Want A Haunted House Torn Down

LOUISVILLE- The residents in the neighborhood of Twenty-sixth and St. Cecelia Streets, near the old St. John's Cemetery, long since filled, have filed a request with Inspector Tilford to tear down the walls of a two-story brick house standing at the intersection of those streets. The grounds for complaint are that the house is haunted, and that children can not be made to pass within a square of the place.

The house was built in 1850, and was occupied by the keepers of the cemetery. The last occupants, the Ziegler family, left it twenty years ago, and said they would

not live in it for $1000 and the rent free. Since that time it has been a rendezvous for thieves, who were evidently not afraid of ghosts.

Many stories of white figures, unearthly yells, moans, etc., have been told, and even so reputable an officer as Captain Kremer testified to having seen a shape in white flitting bout the vacant rooms at 3 o'clock one morning. Inspector Tilford says he has no authority to tear down the house, and referred the complaints to Chief of Police Haager. He, too disclaims authority in the matter, ghosts being a little out of his class. They will, therefore be allowed to revel at their own sweet will.

—*Dallas Morning News*
February 13, 1898

❖ ❖ ❖

The Second Ward Ghost
Singular Experiences With A Supernatural Visitor Related By J. Hamilton Brown. This Ghost Defies The Police. Mr. Brown Just Dotes On Ghosts, He Says, But Was Given A Disappointment Last Night.

DALLAS- A young man calling himself J. Hamilton Brown occupies a one-story cottage over in the second ward north of Pacific Avenue. He called at *The News* office yesterday and stated that he was the owner of a mystery—a ghost—who made nightly visitations and vociferations to his cottage. A News representative promised to call and investigate and at 8:30 o'clock last night the ghost editor was dispatched to the "hant" of the supernatural visitor. He found the place described by Mr. J. Hamilton Brown and a loud knock brought that party to the door. He was in high glee and did not act like a man whose dreams had been broken by the clammy touch of a bloodless and formless apparition from another country.

"I am so sorry," he began, "but I fear that the ghost will not show up to-night. You see he was due at 7:30 o'clock and it is nearly 9 o'clock now. I visited *The News* office to-day and extended an invitation to the staff to come over here and meet the ghost to-night. His plans have been upset, I fear, and he has gone elsewhere to-night."

"Just my darned luck," muttered the ghost editor. "I am a Jonah. Whenever I visit a 'hant' the ghost jumps out and away and the visitations and vociferations are suspended. Say, is your ghost a male or female courier from the spirit world?" "A male ghost of course. This ghost has a piping voice like a boy of 18 years. He called just about two weeks ago and we had a very animated conversation. You see, I am not afraid of ghosts and rather enjoyed a visit from this one. I 'jollied' him a good bit, but he never indulged in a laugh or even cracked a smile at my jokes. Sunday night he came about 8 o'clock and rapped on the wall. We had a chat and jollied him again. He didn't appreciate my 'jollying' qualities, however. He did not laugh once which demonstrates that his ghostship is a most patient listener. He grew ugly and threatening and I went out and hunted up a policeman. The ghost retired for the night. Monday night he came back at the usual

hour and cut up some more pranks. He didn't like what I had to say and gave fair warning that he would return at 1 o'clock Tuesday morning and kill the inmates of the house. I went out again and returned with seven police officers. We made a most sweeping investigation, but the ghost refused to materialize. The police officers were unable to solve the mystery."

The ghost editor of *The News* waited an hour or more, but the privileges of meeting the ghost and interviewing him anent the condition of things in the spirit world was denied the scribe. No ghost appeared. Mr. J. Hamilton Brown expressed his sincere disgust at the refusal of the ghost to come forth and promised to send a messenger to *The News* office in the event that the ghost sneaked in after the departure of *The News* representative. On this earth the ghost was a lightning rod agent, it is understood, and has a great grievance against the managing editor of the spirit world because the game of dominoes is prohibited over there.

—*Dallas Morning News*
February 16, 1898

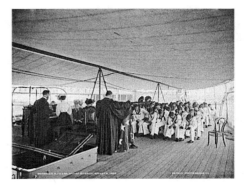

Farmhouse Haunted
Spook In Menard County
That Occasions Much Excitement

MENARDVILLE- On the farm of W.W. Lewis, two and one-half miles east of Menardville, there is reported to be a haunted house. The alleged spook takes the form of a very old woman, with long streaming hair and arms of extreme length, which she waves in a peculiar manner, seemingly to frighten those bold enough to invade her premises and at the same time beating the walls and floor of her dwelling with some invisible instrument, supposed to be a tomahawk. The spook is believed to be the squaw of some departed brave. She has a particular love for men and boys, caressing and embracing them while asleep, and when the victim of her fond embrace would wake up and attempt to return the compliment he would find that the ghost was gone and that the was holding on to blank space only.

No one can stay in the house at midnight because this hobgoblin keeps a continuous noise, imitating the hoot of an owl and the howl of a wolf. With all this the ghost at times is friendly, having often extended its hands for a handshake.

The above comes from responsible parties, the truth of which is vouchsafed by many residents of this county. Near the location of this house is an ancient burying ground, all buried in a sitting posture. It is suggested that this spook is not satisfied with the taking off and came back to finish the job.
—*Dallas Morning News*
April 15, 1901

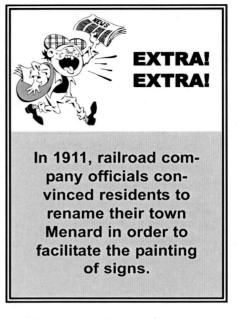

EXTRA! EXTRA!

In 1911, railroad company officials convinced residents to rename their town Menard in order to facilitate the painting of signs.

Firemen Fear Spooks
Mysterious Alarm Comes In
From Box 41.
Key Not Used.

DALLAS- Firemen are beginning to be afraid of spooks, so they say. Yesterday morning about 9:30 the fire bells rang and every indicator in the recorded 41. When the run was made to the corner of Ervay and Park Streets, the box had not been touched and no one knew of a cause for the summons. Thinking there might have been something wrong with the strokes, as the wires in the building are undergoing some repairs, the fireman called up every box that could be made with five strokes, 113, 23, 32, 131, 14, 311, but all no purpose.
—*Dallas Morning News*
September 23, 1903

Hills Prairie Haunted House

HILLS PRAIRIE- Negroes in the neighborhood are very much excited over a haunted house for almost two weeks now. Every night about dusk rock began falling on the roof or gallery and continues until bed time, when probably the ghost get tired. The man's wife died a few months ago and they think she has come back to worry him some more.

—*The Galveston Daily News*
August 2, 1907

❖ ❖ ❖

Mayor Orders Ghost Captured
Special Force Assigned To Seize Figure In Black Which Has Excited Temple

TEMPLE- The ghost scare that has worried the residents of the northern portion of the city for the past two weeks has reached such an acute stage that Mayor Ginnuth has detailed a special force of four extra officers to patrol that section of the city at night and to spare no efforts to get at the bottom of the mystery. It is thought that the work may be that of boys, resident in the neighborhood, who do not realize the danger they are invoking to themselves or the unrest and uneasiness they are causing the ladies and children of the vicinity by their pranks.

Mayor Ginnuth is determined to put a stop to any masquerading that is being carried on, and in this he is strongly supported by

Cameron

CAMERON- While coming from a luncheon at McCown Bridge on Little River, a few miles from here, Thursday night, some young people, while passing an old cemetery, affirm that they saw a wild man or ghost of some kind in the cemetery. A party went in search of the supposed ghost or wild man, but failed to find him although they found a yearling. The parties report that the ghost or wild man was jumping off of the tombstones and making gyrations around there promiscuously.

—*The Galveston Daily News*
September 17, 1905

 ❖ ❖ ❖

PAGE 41

public sentiment. The ghost is garbed in black and its uncanny appearance frightens all passersby.

—*Dallas Morning News*
July 8, 1908

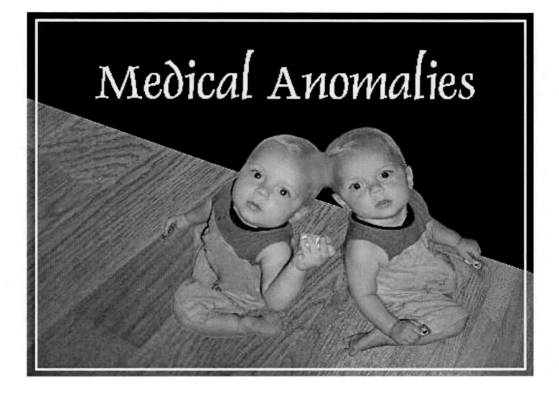

Medical Anomalies

Loses Her Mind From Grief

CLEBURNE- The wife of one of the negroes killed by lightning about a week ago has become insane, and was found this morning walking about in the graveyard aimlessly calling for him. She is also reported to have been seen walking all over the southern portion of the city in the same manner. Her husband's name was Nathan Crawford, and they had only been married about six weeks.

—*Dallas Morning News*
June 2, 1887

❖❖❖

A Family Of Six Persons
With Seventy-two Fingers And Toes Between Them

CISCO- C.J. Johnson of this place presents a curious freak of nature. He has six fingers and six toes on each hand and foot. His brother W.F. Johnson is affected in the same way. He also has two children and a sister that has six fingers and six toes on each hand and foot. Mr. Johnson says his father had the same number as he has.

—*Dallas Morning News*
February 2, 1888

EXTRA! EXTRA!

This condition of having six digits is called hexadactyly.

Insane From Religious Excitement

HILLSBORO- Mrs. Jerry W. Yarbro of this county was adjudged to be of unsound mind in the county court this morning and insanity papers were issued to have her conveyed to the asylum at Terreli. This lady is the wife of one of Hill County's most prominent and influential citizens. She first displayed symptoms of insanity about one month ago, but her reason was not entirely dethroned until Friday last. Religious excitement brought about this result.

—Dallas Morning News
April 19, 1888

❖ ❖ ❖

A Freak Of Nature
A Colored Man Originally Very Black Gradually Becoming White

GALVESTON- The Rev. Thomas Cole, pastor of the East Dallas Street Methodist Episcopal Church at Houston, is in the city attending the colored Sunday school convention. The Rev. Cole is the victim of a very peculiar freak of nature, and from being a black man by birth is rapidly turning white. He says the change began to first manifest itself in 1883, when he was working for the late Dr. McClanahan of this city. It first appeared as a little white pot on the wrist. Since then the white surface began to enlarge and has spread all over his body in spots of various dimensions, from seven inches in length to three and four inches in width down to spots not larger than the circumference of a large sized bird shot. He says his body is stripped like a zebra. His hands are nearer white than black, and his face is beginning to turn, making him a very conspicuous object.

He being naturally very black in color the contrast is all the more striking. As he is attracting a good deal of public attention and being avoided as a leper, he called at *The News* office last night to ask that the statement be made that his physical peculiarity is the result of a freak of nature, and not caused by disease. He has always been perfectly healthy and has never suffered the least physical inconvenience in consequence of this peculiar freak that nature is playing upon him.

—Dallas Morning News
July 16, 1889

❖ ❖ ❖

HIDDEN HEADLINES of TEXAS

A Freak Of Nature

GALVESTON- Editor Bailey of the *Herald* to-day discovered a freak of nature in the shape of a baby white and black, the colors almost equally divided on its body, but having negro parents. It was discovered on Robin Street in the Fourth Ward south.

—*Galveston Daily News*
September 29, 1889

❖ ❖ ❖

Became Suddenly Insane

WORTHAM- Fred Treffinger, a German who had been working with Mr. J.P. Davis, a farmer near this place, became suddenly insane a few days since and was taken to Fairfield to be turned over to the county authorities.

—*Dallas Morning News*
March 22, 1890

❖ ❖ ❖

Made Him Insane
How Somebody's Feigned Joke Frightened A Man Into Insanity

DECATUR- A man by the name of W.S. Sorrells, living near Chico, in this county, was tried yesterday on a charge of insanity and was found to be insane. He appears to be a man of considerable intelligence when he is not in one of his insane spells which seem to come on about dark. About two years ago he and a young man were riding along a public road when several parties who were secreted by the roadside

discharged their pistols and his companion fell from his horse apparently dead. Mr. Sorrells thinking that they were waylaid, became badly frightened and since that time his mind has been gradually getting worse. And he was all right before that time; it is thought that the scare caused his insanity.

—*Dallas Morning News*
September 11, 1890

EXTRA! EXTRA!

Decatur, Texas is the home to the nation's Guacamole Festival.

Negro Turns White
Joseph McMullen, A Well-to-do Farmer, Astonishes The Natives.

CLEBURNE- There was a negro man to-day attracting a great deal of attention. As soon as the large crowd which had gathered around him dispersed *The News* reporter got him cornered and asked: "What was this crowd gathered around you for, uncle?" While asking the question the reporter's gaze rested for a moment on the negro's hands, and to his astonishment they were as white as a woman's, only a few dark spots about the size of a dime remained on them.

"I am getting to be a white man," replied the Senegambian modestly. On examination part of his face was found to be almost as black as jet, while his hands, arm, forehead and about two-thirds of his body was as white as a lady's skin. It did not have a tinge of copper color about it, but looked like the skin of the purest blooded Caucasian. His scalp was white in spots, and where the white spots were the hair was white also, the other being black as ebony and curly.

His name is Joseph McMullen and he lives in Hill County, five miles west of Milford, where he has a good farm of his own, consisting of 360 acres of black waxy land. He is an intelligent negro, 55 years old last March. He says his skin commenced to turn white in March, 1888, and began on his hands and has been spreading ever since. A very remarkable feature about the whole affair is that the skin does not pull off, but just changes color. He says his health has never been affected in the least by this wonderful freak of nature.

He was brought here as a slave in 1853 by a family named McMullen and has lived in Hill County ever since. He seems very proud of the fact that he is turning white, and if he lives a few years longer he will be as white as a Caucasian and it will be impossible for any one to ascertain that he has a drop of African blood in his veins, as he has clean cut features, an aquiline nose and thin lips.

—Dallas Morning News
May 19, 1892

Demented Over Religion

HILLSBORO- Mrs. Nellie Hunter, living near Abbott, on trial before Judge Cunningham to-day, was adjudged insane and ordered taken to the asylum. She became demented on the subject of religion.

—Dallas Morning News
September 5, 1894

❖ ❖ ❖

He, She, Or It?

SAN ANTONIO- The above title refers to one of the most remarkable freaks of nature that have ever been seen or heard of. It is a human being, which is alive and possesses the arms, breasts, hips, legs and feet of a woman. Physicians have been unable to say that this strange being is either male or female. The voice and manner are feminine, but as there are no sexual developments the medical fraternity has been unable to classify this case of malformation in his or her proper category.

Nature here manifests itself in a phase bordering on a conflict of sexes, the male and female form divine combined in one body. This living wonder was born in Galveston, Texas, twenty-two years ago, and is now on a tour of the Pacific Coast. This curious being arrived here yesterday and has been privately examined by the following San Antonio physicians, who have given a certificate stating that this is an extraordinary freak of nature and advise anyone interested in nature's handiwork to go and see this living wonder, signed by Dr. Russell

HIDDEN HEADLINES of TEXAS

Caffery, F.E. Young, F.D. Davenport, W.R. Owen, J.E. Clemens, A.D. Dupuy and others. This marvelous being will be on exhibition for gentlemen only for one week, commencing to-day. Doors open from 10 a.m. to 10 p.m. Place of exhibition, 321 West Commerce St. Admission 25¢.

—*San Antonio Daily Light*
March 22, 1895

❖ ❖ ❖

Run Insane By Religion

TAYLOR- Mrs. J.B. Alford of this city, a widow with three small children whose mind became unbalanced through religious excitement during a recent Methodist revival at the tabernacle here, was taken to the insane asylum at Austin this morning.

—*Dallas Morning News*
August 16, 1895

❖ ❖ ❖

Made Crazy By
A Wolf Bite

LAREDO- A goat-herder, who was bitten several days ago by a rabid wolf near San Ignacio, sixty miles below Laredo, became insane and killed three small children before the officers finally overtook him. It was necessary to rope him before he could be brought under subjection. He is now in jail at Carrizo.

—*Dallas Morning News*
September 9, 1900

Were Crazed By
The Storm

TERRELL- Four patients were brought to the asylum here yesterday from Galveston, each one of whom became demented from the awful effects of the Galveston storm, which destroyed all their earthy possessions.

—*Dallas Morning News*
July 1, 1901

❖ ❖ ❖

Injured Man
Coughs Up Bullet

TEMPLE- J.W. Daniel of this city, half-brother of the man Trapp who was shot by an insane man at Brownwood last week, returned from the latter place last week. After his arrival he received a message stating that Mr. Trapp had coughed up the bullet, which was supposed to have lodged against the spinal column and that he is now considered out of danger.

—*Dallas Morning News*
February 2, 1903

CHAPTER 3 MEDICAL ANOMALIES

Nail Found In Heart Of A Cow

BROWNWOOD- Not many are willing to believe the statement, but it is a fact nevertheless, that a ten-penny nail was sticking through the heart of a cow killed for beef by one of the local butchers. The nail was on the inside of the heart and one end of it was bright while the other was rusty.

The bright part of the nail was sticking in the lower part of the heart about an inch deep. How the nail came there no one can tell, but those who viewed the wonder have advanced various theories in an effort to solve the mystery. The most plausible theory advanced is that the cow swallowed the nail and in some way it worked into a blood vessel and was carried by force to the flowing blood of the heart. When once inside the heart it gradually worked its way through the membranes.

The brightness of one end of the nail is accounted for by the reason of the constant flow of blood through the heart. It matter not how it came there, but it is a great wonder that anything could live with a big ten-penny nail sticking half way through the heart. A local physician examined the heart and said why death was not produced is a baffling question to him. The butcher informs us that the cow was as fine and fat as any stall-fed cow in the country.

—*Dallas Morning News*
July 16, 1905

❖ ❖ ❖

EXTRA! EXTRA!

A ten-penny nail is 3.0 inches long and got its name due to the cost per hundred.

Found In Dazed Condition
Jess O. Charles, An Operator, Later Becomes Delirious.

DALLAS- Jess O. Charles, a telegraph operator lately in Dallas from Rhome, was found on the streets yesterday in a dazed condition that later became delirious. He was conveyed to the City Hall. In a very short time he had lost consciousness and in fear that he was dying or dead, the Chief of Police sent for the City Health Officer. Dr. A.W. Nash responded. He declared that the man had been heavily "doped" and that it would be several days before he would be able to work.

The motive for the "doping" is a mystery to the police. Nothing was taken from the man who had on his person a considerable amount of money.

—*Dallas Morning News*
July 29, 1907

Mysterious Creatures

Mysterious Creatures
A Texas Monster
For The Ohio Bear Story

WHITEWRIGHT- A puma which has been infesting the neighborhood of Pilot Grove for several weeks, yesterday tore to pieces and devoured the two-year-old child of a farmer living on the Burns tract. Nothing was left of the child by the beast but the fleshless bones. The puma has been seen several times in North Texas.

—*Dallas Morning News*
July 11, 1880

❖ ❖ ❖

Got What He Went For

GALVESTON- A reporter observed a photographer this morning, with his battery planted in front of Mr. Baldwin's City Livery stable, on Fannin Street, and immediately went for an item, and got what he went for. The artist was taking the counterfeit presentment of a mule, or jennet, that presents a freak of nature, as strange as we ever saw in a menagerie or a museum. It is natural enough in its general build, proportions, and appearances, but its two fore feet are shaped like human feet or rather like a pair of India rubber slippers, and its hind feet are about eighteen inches long, and project in a spiral coil, and look like a compromise between a ram's horn and an elephant's trunk. While the reporter was there, Dr. D.F. Stuart came up and examined the animal, and joined in the general idea that it is a strange freak of nature. We understand that the proprietors of several northern museums have written to Mr. Baldwin to know what he will take for his remarkable mule.

—*The Galveston Daily News*
May 17, 1883

❖ ❖ ❖

A Texas Monster
Birth Of A Freak Half Human And Half Centipede, At Eagle Pass.
[From the *Eagle Pass Maverick*]

EAGLE PASS- An attaché of the Maverick, while wandering around town the other evening in quest of something which might satiate the cravings of the reading world, overheard a conversation which opened the avenue to a startling item, and, with the object of getting at the details, he approached one of the party, who is a physician, and made inquiry as to the conversation overheard a few moments previous, but was meant with a blunt but polite refusal to be let any farther into the secret: but after a dogged persistence on the part of the Maverick representative, the gentleman approached agreed to conduct him to the seclusion of the monstrosity, he first agreeing to give neither name nor locality. Accordingly, in company with the attending physician he visited the house, where was found to his utter astonishment, a human deformity the like of which the mind is scarcely capable of conceiving. This curiosity is three days old, weighs five and a half pounds, has a well devel-

oped head, but no sign of hair, and when viewing it in a dark room with a lighted lamp it seems to be perfectly transparent, an object on the opposite side of the head being easily distinguished, and what appears to be the brain is constantly moving, not even ceasing when the child (if such as it can be called) appears to be sleeping. The body, as low down as the hips is well developed and symmetrically formed, but the legs, feet, arms and hands have the exact counterparts of the centipede, the fingers and toes resembling the claws of one of those reptiles, and are of a fleshy substance, but have been growing harder ever since birth. The toes and fingers are also transparent, being of a light reddish color, and are ever and often on the move. Should this nondescript live, it will prove to be the greatest curiosity ever known to anatomy.

The mother, who is of more than ordinary intelligence, expresses great sorrow at the phenomenal deformity of her offspring, and appears to have all the maternal love and care that is usually bestowed upon those more fortunate, and desires that it live, but says the world remain in ignorance as to it maternity.

Should this freak of nature show evidences of living we will be permitted to write more fully of it at another time, but by request we will say no more of it at present.

—*The Galveston Daily News*
March 24, 1884

HIDDEN HEADLINES of TEXAS

Natural Monstrosity

GALVESTON- A natural monstrosity, in the shape of a young calf with seven legs and eight feet, was being exhibited to-day as a natural curiosity. The animal was born dead several miles from the city.

—*The Galveston Daily News*
May 31, 1884

❖ ❖ ❖

Rather A Steep Story

GALVESTON- Mr. W.H. Bailey, of the Herald, has brought to light a strange specimen of malformation. This is his description of it: A most wonderful curiosity in the shape of a pig with a head something like a dog's and a tail resembling that of a horse, was thrown to a reporter of the Herald this morning. This strange monstrosity is about a week old and is in a healthy condition. It belongs to an old colored woman named Martha Simpson, living in the Fourth Ward, south. A number of people visited her house yesterday to get a glimpse of the animal.

When the reporter arrived it was quietly grazing near the house. The owner stated that it would eat nothing but grass, positively refusing to touch anything else. Occasionally it would raise its head and bray like a donkey. Several scientific gentlemen have seen it, but all have failed to come to any definite conclusion concerning it. A combination of dog, pig and jackass would be apt to down the analytical powers of the most learned scientist. When the combination brays and eats grass then it is simply startling—in fact immense. Let up, Mr. Bailey, Hamp Cook is out of town.

—*The Galveston Daily News*
June 7, 1885

❖ ❖ ❖

A Wild Man

DALLAS- Tom Botter, who lives in the neighborhood of Miller Crossing, on Elm Fork, came to the County Attorney's office yesterday evening and wanted advice. He said that an Italian by the name of John Spiengy, living near him, had become insane a few days ago. He had been running through the woods, climbing tress and refusing any nourishment. An effort had been made to catch him, but, as he would not go in a house and was fleet of foot, all efforts in that direction were futile. He imagines that he is pursued by men who want to kill him, and he runs away whenever he sees anyone. Botter filed a complaint, and a warrant was issued that he may be tried for lunacy. As he is poorly dressed, fears are expressed that if he is not caught the present cold nights may cause his death.

—*Dallas Morning News*
October 21, 1885

EXTRA! EXTRA!

Texas is the only state to fly flags from six different countries. The flags are from the Republic of Texas, Spain, Mexico, United States, France, and the Confederate States.

A Monstrosity

WEATHERFORD- A monstrosity was born in Parker County a few days ago, that seemed to be part pig, part elephant and part human. It only lived a few minutes, but is preserved in alcohol, and can be seen in Weatherford.

—*San Antonio Light*
March 20, 1888

❖ ❖ ❖

A Huge Wolf Killed
Big As A Yearling

LEONARD- Frank Boshore, a farmer living near the city, killed and brought to town yesterday one of the largest gray wolves that was ever killed in this country. It was nearly as tall as a yearling calf. These animals have been a great disadvantage to the community, one man saying that he had been damaged at least $1000 by them on sheep.

—*Dallas Morning News*
June 2, 1888

A Freak Of Nature

GALVENSTON- A gentleman from the country this morning was exhibiting to curious citizens an odd natural freak in the shape of an opossum of more than usual size, and possessing all the well-defined facial features of an infant. The ears, nose, forehead and chin are well developed and shapely, but the even and symmetrical development of the animal in its alliance to the human family is marred by the member which Darwin credited to our early parents—a tail. Its voice somewhat resembles that of the suppressed sobs of a babe. It is a curious looking creature and will probably be purchased and exhibited by some of our scientific townsmen.

—*The Galveston Daily News*
August 2, 1888

❖ ❖ ❖

Monster Tape Worm

HILLSBORO- A physician of this city recently removed a tape worm 40 feet in length from the stomach of a little 3-year-old child of this city. The little one had been in wretched health for some time but is now improving rapidly.

—*Dallas Morning News*
July 20, 1889

❖ ❖ ❖

A Big Alligator

OAK CLIFF- A monster alligator may be seen at Oak Cliff. The reptile is ten feet in length and possesses a set of teeth that is very suggestive. The monster was caught about ten days ago at Bois d'arc Island in the Trinity, twenty-five miles from Dallas, by S.D. Matherson and John Cranch, who brought it to Oak Cliff in a wagon. The alligator was first discovered in a hole or cave on the island, and after persuading him to thrust his heard forth, the two men lassoed him and drew him out. It is pronounced among the largest that have ever been caught in the Trinity.

—*Dallas Morning News*
August 30, 1891

❖ ❖ ❖

Encounter A Wild Man

SAN ANTONIO- Mr. George Cole and Jimmie Hightower returned Thursday from a ten day fish and hunt in the bottoms of the San Antonio River in Refugle County, about forty miles from Golind.

Mr. Coles relates an adventure which he had while gone with a wild man of the forest. "We saw coming towards us on the opposite side of the river, what appeared to be a man of about 60 years of age. His beard and hair were long and wavy and he was almost entirely nude, his only articles of clothing being sandals upon his feet and a turban-like hat upon his head. His body was covered with a thick growth of black, shaggy hair. He walker erect with his arms folded upon his breast, and came within 60 or 100 yards of us. Our presence did not seem to startle him in the least. I called to him in English, Spanish, and French, but he paid no attention whatsoever and calmly continued his walk up the river bank." Mr. Cole remained near this spot for several days, but saw no more of this strange being.

A party should be organized to go for this wild man of the woods about April 1.

—*The Galveston Daily News*
March 22, 1892

❖ ❖ ❖

A Freak of Nature

CLEBURNE- A freak of nature is reported from near Grandview, where a mare belonging to a Mr. Hill gave birth to twins, one being a horse and the other a mule colt. Both are living.

—*Dallas Morning News*
April 6, 1892

❖ ❖ ❖

CHAPTER 4 MYSTERIOUS CREATURES

A Freak Like A Turtle

MARSHALL- A mulatto woman living near here gave birth to a freak resembling a turtle. It is a female about eight inches long and apparently healthy. Its head and face are those of a human being, while the balance of its body is like that of an animal. The nails are like claws while the body is covered with hair.

—*The Galveston Daily News*
July 13, 1892

❖ ❖ ❖

Shot A Huge Devilfish
It Measured Fourteen Feet From Tip To Tip.
Three Galveston Boys Captured The Monster.

GALVESTON- Yesterday sea devils were to be seen sporting around the third bar at the beach in front of the Pagoda. The sea devil or devil fish white ray or sea bat, if you will, bears the name of *lophius piscatorious.*

Louis and Stanley Sinclair and Joe McNamara—none of them being more than 16 years old—saw these fishes and determined to get one and sell it. So one of the boys borrowed a Winchester rifle while the other two got a row boat and a harpoon. And out they went for their prey.

The devil fish is reputed to be of a sluggish disposition—like all gluttons. It feeds, as a rule, at the bottom of the sea, in the mud, attracting its prey by waving its tentacles—they are silvery looking—and thereby exciting the curiosity of small fishes. In swimming near the surface this fish sticks the tip of one wing out of the water and moves along slowly unless startled, in which event a locomotive can not keep it in sight: the speed which the fish can develop has been estimated at more than sixty miles an hour, and that goes to show about how sluggish such a fish is.

The boys rowed around and soon saw one of the fishes—the devil fish is not easily frightened—and pulled up within forty or fifty feet. Joe McNamara fired a shot into the ray, which immediately breached, scooting fully twenty feet out and ahead like a flying fish. Two more shots were fired, and after beating the water into flinders, it died. Then a harpoon was thrown into the fish and it was towed to O'Keefe's where it was slung and hoisted out with a windlass. It was then put on a float and hauled over to the Beach Hotel, where it can be seen at any time by those who have the curiosity to go there.

The fish measures 14 feet from wing tip to wing tip. Its mouth is an arc of about 260 degrees. Such fish are common off Tampa, where they at times create consternation among the fishermen at anchor by running afoul of a hawser of anchor chain. Closing their nippers or claws thereon and starting for deep water like a runaway locomotive, towing the boat along. Usually in such a case the chain or hawser is slipped or cut, and the fish allowed to go free. The devil fish is captured by harpooning, and even then the sport is dangerous from the possibility of towing under or capsizing. They are not common in these waters.

Colonel Sinclair asked Louis how much he wanted for his prize.

Louis scratched his head and replied, "I'll tell you what, father, take the hotel receipts for this day last year, and those for to-day and give us the difference."

The colonel was thunderstruck, but he rallied somewhat, and had partially recovered from the shock when *The News* reporter saw him last night. It has been suggested that the *lophius piscatorious* be adopted as the coat of arms of the campaign orator, on account of its leathery mouth and sluggish nature.

—*Dallas Morning News*
August 19, 1892

❖ ❖ ❖

Thought It The Devil

VELASCO- The Galveston News recently contained an account of two elks being found in Kansas. Peradventure they got there as an elk did to Bell County, Texas in 1874 or thereabouts.

A party of immigrants from Missouri camped on Little River a few miles below Belton, and lost a pet elk in the woods. He was a monster fellow, with a full set of antlers. After searching vainly for their pet, the immigrants continued their journey west. In those days Bell County had no railroads, and freight was brought by wagon from Calvert. About a week after the elk was lost a train of a dozen freighters camped for the night near the river. After supper the teamsters gathered in a circles around a fire to engage in, or watch, a stiff poker game. As the weather was cool, the bottle circulated freely. Suddenly an enormous bearded head with seven foot horns, was thrust over the shoulders of some of the players, and a terrible snort was heard. The entire party of teamsters arose as one man and fled swiftly into outer darkness. Teams, wagons and weapons were not thought of.

Next morning most of the party turned up at farm houses, two to four miles distant from camp, and each one had a different description of the horrible monster that had attacked them. They were a day or two finding some of their stampeded mules. The neighborhood was greatly excited and a general hunt was agreed upon. Just as a courier was being dispatched to Waco with an invitation to General Sul Ross and his bear dogs, the elk appeared on the edge of the timber and sedately walked into a farmer's horse lot, where he was shot. No one would eat the meat, as they did not know what kind of animal it was.

Several moths afterwards one of the Missourians passed through Belton, and accidentally hearing of the circumstances told of having lost his pet elk. In the meantime half of the teamsters had joined the church the first chance they had, and several of their first dolmen vows to reform were made while racing out of Little River bottom, thinking the devil was after them.

—*Dallas Morning News*
November 23, 1893

CHAPTER 4 MYSTERIOUS CREATURES

A Human Fish
Brenham Texas Special

BURTON- News of a strange freak of nature comes from Burton, a small town in the western part of Washington County. To-day a colored woman, attended by Dr. Laas, gave birth to a child, the trunk of which bore a striking resemblance to a red snapper. The lower limbs were perfectly natural and well developed. The attending physician offered a large sum for the specimen, which he desired to preserve but the parents would not let him have it. The colored people who viewed the monstrosity fled in great alarm, and the community is greatly excited over it. They declare the mother to have been hoodooed or conjured.

—*San Antonio Daily Light*
April 18, 1894

❖ ❖ ❖

A Small Horse

SAN ANTONIO- Col. J.H. Wood who purchased the entire stock of Shetland ponies owned by Byron Van Raub about four years ago, is exhibiting a freak in the shape of a full grown horse, known to be the smallest in the world, it being but 19 inches high and weighing 24 pounds. He has named her Baby Ruth after President Cleveland's daughter. Winnie D., another Shetland pony, is also on exhibition and has carried off numerous premiums wherever shown. Both are Texas raised. They will be taken to Europe next month.

—*San Antonio Daily Light*
March 8, 1895

Monster Wild Cat

DENISON- Tom Crowder of Pottsboro captured a monster wildcat in the bottoms. The cat measured five feet two inches from tip to tip.

—*Dallas Morning News*
March 14, 1896

❖ ❖ ❖

Freak Of Nature

SAN ANTONIO- Gus Wagenfuehr, of 1524 of South Presa Street, was the possessor of a freak of nature last Tuesday in the shape of a calf, which had a bull dog head and only one eye. The animal lived but a few minutes.

—*San Antonio Daily Light*
September 24, 1896

❖ ❖ ❖

Eighteen-Horn Cow

TAYLOR- A freak of nature from the animal kingdom in the way of a cow with eighteen horns is now on exhibition in Taylor. Ten of her horns measure in varying lengths from ten to twenty inches, representing the horns of the cow, the goat and the sheep, while the eight smallest horns form a representation of the calf, the kid and the lamb. This freak excites considerable curiosity.

—*The Galveston Daily News*
May 13, 1897

❖ ❖ ❖

Freak Of Nature

GROESBECK- J.T. Freeman who lives about seven miles west of town on J.C. Sanders' farm, brought into town this morning a freak of nature. It was a pig: the frame was perfect, the head contained no eyes and resembled the head of a human being in shape. The nose was a but of flabby flesh, but had no nostril. The mouth was as perfect as that of an infant, having the tongue also in its perfectness. The two fore feet were covered with toes, eleven on each foot, resembling the human fingers very much, though they were without nails. The hind feet resembled the human hand, having five fingers or toes on each foot, each toe having a perfect nail. The hide or skin covering the body was smooth as that of a human being. The people who witnessed this freak of nature noticed in an instant the resemblance of a human being.

—*Dallas Morning News*
July 30, 1899

❖ ❖ ❖

Captured
A Monster Centipede

PARIS- While R.R. Allen, a farmer, living in the Glory community, was coming to town yesterday afternoon he captured a monster centipede crossing the road. It was nearly an inch broad and measured seven inches in length.

—*Dallas Morning News*
October 20, 1899

Freak Of Nature

PARIS- A sow on the farm of Mr. Argyle Wynne, four miles southeast of Paris, gave birth to a litter of pigs, four of which have snouts like an elephant's trunk growing out of their foreheads and extending down below the nose. Three of the pigs died in a few hours. The fourth pig lived four days.
—*Dallas Morning News*
October 24, 1899

❖ ❖ ❖

Sea Serpent
Has Been Seen
Capt. Christiansen Of The Tug
Charles Clarke Passed It
In The Gulf Friday

GALVESTON- The sea serpent has been seen in the gulf. Captain Gus Christiansen of the tug Charles Clarke reports that while on the way to Horn Island with a tow of a mud scow, a dredge and another vessel for the work there, he passed within forty feet of the reptile and was able to get a good view of it. There was no gun aboard, and no camera, so ocular evidence of what was seen can not be given, but he says he is not fabricating, and cites Mr. Robert Clark, of the firm, who was aboard, as a witness to what he says.

"We were about off Pass a l'Outre last Friday, at the mouth of the Mississippi River, when I sighted the thing coming toward us lazily. I called Mr. Clark, who was in the cabin reading, and he came up into the wheel house with me. He took the glasses, and from the upper deck scrutinized the serpent carefully. It was apparently about seventy-five feet long. Long fins protruded from the surface of the water, which was very calm and resembled a sea of glass. It had flippers on the side with which it propelled itself. We could not see its head, which was evidently under water. It was moving in a westerly direction and we were proceeding eastwardly. Therefore we passed each other, and as we passed the serpent was not more than fifty feet away from us. While it seemed to be moving lazily, yet it was going swiftly, propelling itself with its side fins or flippers. It was apparently not at all alarmed at our presence, but kept moving as it had done when we first sighted it. The wake that it left in the quiet water extended for a long distance in the rear of it. It was as great as an ordinary steamer would make. We had no gun aboard, or we might have taken a shot at it."

Captain Christiansen says that the Charles Clarke made a fine run from Horn Island. It is a distance of about 375 miles and was made in twenty-nine hours, which is as good as the average tramp steamer can make when she has all her parts working easily after being in use a year or two.

The serpent story brought out other tales of the demons of the deep. It was told in the presence of several pilots, among others to Captain Carrol, who added the following to his list of published tales of the experiences of the deep. "One day last summer when I was out with the pilot boat Mamie Higgins, and business was dull, I took the dinky and pulled over to the south jetty to fish. I had all the fish I cared to catch, and got back into the dinky to row back to the steamer. I had hardly taken the oars when the most horrible thing I ever saw in water came up and made for me. I jumped out and got onto the jetty as quickly as possible. I was scared, I can tell you. When the thing had passed I took the dinky and went back to the pilot boat. I told Captain Luth of what I had seen. He got his six-shooter and we returned. The thing appeared again, but he was so excited he could not make a good shot and it got away."

"It was the queerest looking thing I ever saw. It had its mouth open and it looked as big as the barrel there. (The barrel was an ordinary apple barrel.) It appeared to be all head. From the back of the head was a sort of long horn or tail as big around a that iron post supporting the awning, and the body was covered with green hair, I never saw a fish before with the tail sticking out of its head."

Captain Wilson verified the statement: "That is right. I was there at the time and remember the incident. There is no joke about it." What Captain Carrol saw was possibly the monster known as a devil fish. It is called the "vampire of the ocean," and is the nearest thing that comes to the description given by Captain Carrol. The species is not numerous and is reported to be rather timid. A specimen was captured near Delaware bay in 1823 which required the combined efforts of three pairs of oxen, a horse and several men to drag it ashore. It weighed about five tons, and was seventeen feet and a half long and eighteen feet wide. The skin on the back was blackish brown and the mouth measured tow and three-fourths feet wide, and the greatest breadth of the skull five feet and the distance between the eyes four and one-sixth feet. The width being greater than the length is accounted for by the presence of huge cartilaginous appendages not unlike wings with which it make progress through the water. This fish is occasionally seen on the coasts of the southern states in summer and autumn. They are not uncommon in the West Indies.

One was captured in 1828 off Jamaica which had a mouth twenty-seven inches wide opening into a cavity four and a half feet wide and three feet deep, large enough to receive the body of a man. The gullet is small so that it is probable that it feeds on nothing but small fry, the large mouth being used to catch its prey, the wings being used when the animal is at rest to draw water towards it, thus sucking in unwary fish. The body is huge and ends in a long tail well armed, which it could use with terrible effect if it had to defend itself. In some species it has two extensions near the eyes which resemble horns. The huge wings in certain positions might give rise to the belief that the animal was covered with hair, especially to a man, who was not acting in the interest of science. These wings, too, if extended upward from the body when the fish was coming directly towards a man might be mistaken for the big horns described by Captain Carrol, as he could see nothing but the front and largest edge.

—*Dallas Morning News*
October 26, 1899

❖ ❖ ❖

A Monster Rattlesnake

CORSICANA- Hon. George T. Jester brought in from his Richland bottom farm to-day the rattles of a monster rattlesnake that was killed on his place by one of his tenants yesterday. In the set there were nineteen rattles and a button and as the reptile never sprouts rattles until he is 3 years old, and one each year thereafter, this would indicate that the snake was 23 years old. Mr. Jester measured the reptile and gave the measurement at 7 feet 4 inches in length and 32 inches in circumference at the thickest part., or nearly eleven inches in diameter. This, so far as *The News* correspondent has been able to learn, is the largest rattlesnake ever killed in this county.

—*Dallas Morning News*
November 1, 1899

❖ ❖ ❖

An Ox Freak

TEXARKANA- A curiosity was seen on exhibition in this city to-day, it being an ox that had one arm projecting from the shoulder blade, about two feet long. The limb has an elbow and a hand containing six claws, all faculties of the member resembling very much those of a human being. The animal belongs to a farmer near this place.

—*Dallas Morning News*
November 4, 1899

Caddo Lake is the only natural lake in the state.

Enormous Mule

DENTON- A mule that would grace a side show on account of its great size was in a local wagon yard to-day. The animal was certainly a freak as far as size goes, and the head was enormously large even for the great size of the other parts of the body. *The News* correspondent is a half inch over six feet tall, and when he stood by the side of the mule the latter towered above his fully four inches.

—*Dallas Morning News*
November 7, 1899

❖ ❖ ❖

Cows Attacked
A Wild Beast Bit Her
In A Lot On Leal Street

SAN ANTONIO- Some ferocious wild beast, believed to have been either a wild cat, panther or Mexican lion, attacked a cow belonging to a man named Wander, on Leal Street yesterday morning at 1o'clock and bit the animal several times in the neck. It was frightened off, however, before the cow was killed. The cow has since died. Her calf which she was defending was killed.

—*San Antonio Daily Light*
January 8, 1900

❖ ❖ ❖

Bryan's Panther

SAN ANTONIO- A posse of citizens, headed by the assistant chief of police of San Antonio, the other day chased a panther which had for some time been lurking in the suburbs of the city and depredating in chicken coops. They failed to catch him, having lost the trail in the chaparral, only three miles from the center of the city.

This was not the panther which Mr. Bryan and the citizens ran into a tree and captured alive. The San Antonio panther was wild.

—*The Galveston Daily News*
January 9, 1900

❖ ❖ ❖

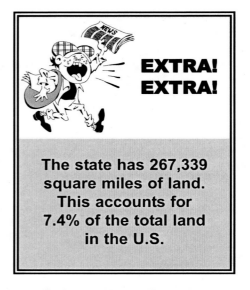

EXTRA! EXTRA!

The state has 267,339 square miles of land. This accounts for 7.4% of the total land in the U.S.

Evidently A Panther
Wild Beast Continues West-side Depredations

SAN ANTONIO- The capture of the bob-tailed wild cat on the Leona Sunday afternoon has not served to make the residents of the west-side rest easy, as it did not rid them of the animal that had recently been disturbing their chicken coops and cow-pens.

As mentioned yesterday, the beast attacked and killed a cow on Leona Street Sunday night and it was back in the sane community last night. About 9:30 o'clock it was seen in the rear yard of the Murphy residence on Ruis Street, and was chased back to Leal Street through the yard of Mr. Wander where it killed the cow the night previous. Here it was almost overtaken by the pursuers—George Rine and Walter O'Brient—and both fired at it; one with a revolver and one with a shotgun but with a howl of rage or pain as if shot, it bounded away and escaped.

The boys had a good look at it, and it was larger than the wild-cats killed Sunday, which lends to the belief that it is a panther as was at first supposed. The beast is believed to have remained in the vicinity and continued his prowl during the rest of the night as fowls were heard making a noise as if disturbed suddenly in various parts of the community the remainder of the night.

—*San Antonio Light*
January 9, 1900

The armadillo is the official state mammal.

One of Nature's Freaks

BONHAM- A freak of nature was found by J.C. Yoakum, near Honey Grove, this week. It was half pig and half calf, the head and body being that of a calf, while the lower jaw, legs and feet were those of a hog. It was dead when found.

—*Dallas Morning News*
February 3, 1901

Wild Man Of The Woods
Farmers Around Santo Have Tried In Vain To Catch Him

SANTO- There is much excitement near Judd Switch because of a negro who seems to be wild or insane. He has been in the neighborhood about two months. About twenty men gathered in the John Morris neighborhood last night and tried to capture him. They found where he had built a fire, but he was not there, and they made a drive for him with hounds, but could not catch him. He can run like a pony. He is perfectly nude, except for something around his waist that reaches down about half way of his things. The people to-morrow will make another effort to catch him.

—*Dallas Morning News*
March 31, 1901

❖ ❖ ❖

Has Queer Monster
Assistant State Geologist Cummins Will Make An Unusual Exhibit At The Fair

DALLAS- Prof. W.F. Cummins, assistant State Geologist and Superintendent of the Geological Department of the Texas State Fair, says that since last year he has added a large number of specimens to his collection at the fair grounds, among them an unclassified reptile which he found in Southwestern Texas. He says it is of the turtle or terrapin family, and it is the nearest approach so far discovered to what all creatures which are protected by a bony or horny exterior casing were evidently tending when they were arrested in their devel-

PAGE 65

opment or evolution, namely, to the point where they could detach themselves from their shell and come out of it, and go back into it, precisely as a person can come out of and go back into a house at pleasure. In other words this reptile could crawl out of its shell when it deemed the coast clear and on the approach of an enemy crawl back into it and shut it up. After the fair Prof. Cummins intends to present this unique reptile to the Smithsonian Institution.

—*Dallas Morning News*
August 16, 1901

❖ ❖ ❖

Killed A Monster Eagle

PYRON- A few days ago while I was off on business, Oscar, my 14-year-old son, was trapping for coyotes. On going to his trap he found an eagle in one of them. When in shotgun range the boy fired on him, when at the crack of the gun the bird rose from the ground flying vigorously toward the boy, dragging trap, chain and weight after him, when the boy emptied the other barrel at him, bringing his to the ground. The trap and weight which were attached to it with a chain weighs thirty-five pounds. The morning of the third day after Mr. F. Wilkerson, proprietor of the Dr. Scarber Hotel of Snyder, and myself measured the bird. It was seven feet eight inches from point to point of his wings, three feet three inches from point to bill to tip of tail and from point of middle toe to the point of back toe exactly eight inches. He is a smutty brown color.

—*Dallas Morning News*
November 18, 1901

EXTRA! EXTRA!

With 6,208 square miles, Brewster is the largest county in Texas.

Horned Rabbits
Horns, It Is Asserted, Are The Result Of A Disease

FARMERS BRANCH- If *The News* will give me space I will explain the mystery about Brother Harnesberger's horned rabbit. I have seen lots of them. In the year 1880 or 1881 I lived with my uncle, Godfrey Baccus on the headwaters of Rowlett Creek in Collin County. In one of these years I saw many horned rabbits. I killed one rabbit on which I counted fourteen horns, and some four or five were on its head. The horns were an inch or more in length and hung down over its eyes, so that it seemed to be almost blind. These horns are caused by a rabbit disease. I think the disease is fatal: I know it was to the ones I saw, for they fell an easy victim to my dogs.

I killed rabbits at this time that had swellings or bumps on them about the size of marbles. This is the first stage of the disease. When these swellings break, the corruption gets on the fur and dries, and thus the horn is formed. There seems to be as many horns as there are bumps on the rabbit. The "horns" are not horns, but only shaped like horns, and are only attached to the skin and fur and not to the bones.

—*Dallas Morning News*
March 14, 1902

❖ ❖ ❖

Captured A Sea Hog
One Weighing About 300 Pounds Landed Near Corpus Christi

CORPUS CHRISTI- The first manatee, or sea hog, ever captured in Corpus Christi waters has been on exhibition here all day. The monster was caught at Corpus Pass and measured over six feet and weighs about three hundred pounds. It was purchased to-day by a local showman, but died after being taken from the water. Old fisherman say they never before heard of a sea hog captured on the Texas coast.

—*Dallas Morning News*
March 28, 1902

❖ ❖ ❖

Wild Lion In Calvert
It Played Havoc With Chickens Until Killed By A Resident

CALVERT- From Alderman C.S. Allen, *The News* correspondent, learns of the story of a thrilling adventure with a Mexican lion a night or so ago in North Calvert. Alderman Allen states the beast had been prowling around in his neighbor-

hood for several nights, playing sad havoc with the chickens, until he drifted into the yard of Lee Horton, who owns two large bull dogs. The dogs attacked the lion and a fierce fight followed, when Mr. Horton appeared on the scene with a shotgun and riddled the ferocious animal with buckshot, but not until the beast had almost killed one of the dogs. Just where the animal came from is a mystery. He is described as a large, ferocious animal, and was evidently driven into town by intense hunger.

—*Dallas Morning News*
February 16, 1903

EXTRA! EXTRA!

More species of bats live in Texas than in any other part of the United States.

Strange Reptile At Paris

PARIS- While E.E. Smither, fireman of the switch engine in the Texas and Pacific yards, was walking along South Jefferson Street near the railroad track this morning his attention was attracted by a strange reptile crawling across the sidewalk. It apparently belongs to the lizard family and in many respects resembles the Gila monster.

Its motions are more sluggish than a lizard's and a little livelier than those of the monster. It was about five inches long, its tail being about as long as its head and body together. Its color is an ashy black, like India rubber, the skin smooth and pulpy, and the belly bluish-black. It holds its head erect and its eyes bulge out. On each side of the center of the back, extending from the head to the end of the tail is a straight row of rough yellow spots of different sizes that look like they might have been daubed with paint by an unartistic brush and unskilled hand.

Fireman Smither captured the reptile by placing an umbrella handle over its head and tied a cord around its tail. It tried to bite the string in two, and in its rage bit it's own flesh. A milky substance oozed from the self-inflicted wound. The reptile was carried to the depot and viewed by scores of persons around the platform waiting for the train. One man said it was a water dog and another said it was a ground puppy. A third said he had seen one of its species before, that it was more poisonous than a rattlesnake, and that its habitat is among rotten logs.

A negro, who claimed that it was a ground puppy, said that "when one of them barks at you, you will die." The strange reptile is believed to have escaped from a carload of bananas shipped to Paris from New Orleans a day or two ago.

—*Dallas Morning News*
April 13, 1903

Big Centipede At Paris

PARIS- Conductor E. S. Lowrance of the Frisco came in on his run this morning with a monster live centipede ten inches long in a big pickle jar. A fisherman at Buck Creek tank, in the Territory, made him a present of it.

—*Dallas Morning News*
April 30, 1903

❖ ❖ ❖

Horned Game Chicken
Strange Freak Of Nature On Exhibition At Eastland

EASTLAND- Cal Yancey, who lives a little way from Eastland, had on exhibition yesterday a strange freak in the nature of a horned game chicken. The chicken had two horns, one about one and one-quarter of an inch long, and the other about one inch. They were hard and protruded, one over each eye. The chicken was in other respects perfect.

—*Dallas Morning News*
May 8, 1903

❖ ❖ ❖

Hunt For Phantom-Like Animal
Waco People Are Puzzled Over Destructive Work Of Living Something That Is Unknown

WACO- An animal described by persons who have seen him in the night as a large, lean dog, has been terrorizing people in the city for a month. It has been known to kill and devour pigs, puppies, ducks, geese and hens. Its most recent exploit was to invade the premises of J.R. Railey, 2210 Austin Avenue, and after eating a few chickens, entered a vacant servant's house through a window, demolishing the mattress and the bed clothing. Last night the animal paid a second visit to Mr. Railey's premises, and finding that the poultry had been placed out of reach, entered the carriage house and from appearances made an attempt to eat up a surrey, chewing the covers off the cushion and tearing the padded sided of the vehicle into shreds.

Mr. Railey was damaged about $30 by the nocturnal, mysterious mammal which the best biologists in the city have so far been unable to classify from examining the footprints, and by the descriptions given by the few people who have seen the intruder passing like a phantom, jumping fences from one lot to another, elusive and shadowy, except where the use is made of teeth and claws. The McLennan County Fox Hunters' Association with their best hunters declare that while they have been able to capture big wolves, red and gray foxes, bob cats and catamounts, they are baffled by this peculiar beast. It is still being hunted. The prevailing belief is that the animal is a dog returned to savagery from having led a vagrant, homeless life.

—Dallas Morning News
January 29, 1908

❖ ❖ ❖

Wild Man

GALVESTON- A supposed wild man is creating consternation in the Charles Steelhammer neighborhood. He visits houses at night or while the families are away and helps himself to whatever his fancy craves. He laps up the cream like a dog and eats fried chicken raw, so they say. A number of citizens of that community sleep in arms and carry their scatter guns and forty-some-odds in their work for fear of being chewed up by this great human monstrosity. He has been seen a number of times, and each time those who saw him describe his manner of running as resembling the lope of a wolf, and not unlike the flight of an airship.

Well, do not be hard on the poor, frenzied, half-famished creature; he is probably some eminent Republican who ran away to keep from being nominated for the vice presidency.

—The Galveston Daily News
June 26, 1908

❖ ❖ ❖

Marvelous Fish
On Exhibition In Electric Park

GALVESTON- The monster unknown by name in the fish world which was caught up on the jetties yesterday, will be on exhibition to-day at the Electric Park.

—The Galveston Daily News
August 21, 1910

A Remarkable Coincidence

DALLAS- If miracles have ceased, the fact that wonderful coincidences still exist was demonstrated yesterday at a furniture store on Elm Street. Two months ago, while one of the clerks was explaining the merits of a derringer pistol to a countryman, and in the act of showing how the spring worked, the little infernal machine, which was supposed to be empty, went off, the ball penetrating the combing of the showcase though the wood and metal.

The clerk thereupon registered a vow that the possibility of a pistol being loaded in his showcase should never occur again.

Yesterday he had occasion to take out the same derringer, and while proving its fine parts to a customer it went off as before, the ball taking the same course and partly entering the hole made by the former accident. The clerk is ready to swear that the pistol could not have been loaded by earthly hands, and the religious conviction given to the matter is that the spirit of some desperado from the summer land had taken quarters in the showcase and put it in rapport with the derringer.

—*Dallas Morning News*
November 22, 1885

A Voodoo Conjuration

**Poe Discounted In Goldbuggery.
A Stringtown Negro Spiritually
Guided Through Golden Visions
To The Calaboose.
A Strange Story.**

DALLAS- Mr. C. M. Terry, on his way home in the southwestern quarter of the city Friday night, espied a dim light in the thicket in the bottom, a short distance beyond the jail. Prompted by curiosity, he went near, to ascertain what it meant. Suddenly the light went out, and there was a sound as if someone was running. Mr. Terry approached the spot whence the light had proceeded and there found a spade and a pick and an excavation in the similitude of a half dug grave. He came back to town and notified Police Officers Pryor and Hatsell, who went down and made an inspection, and in addition to what Mr. Terry saw they found four mule shoes set around the excavation and also a bible a few feet from it. The excavation was about four feet in length by two in width and three deep. On a fly leaf of the bible appeared the name of James Dooling.

The officers enjoyed the acquaintance of a colored man of the name, residing on Boli Street, and to his house they repaired. Dooling responded in person to the knock on the door, and in answer to the query if he were the proprietor of the copy of the inspired word which Officer Pryor held in his hand he said he was. He also made an affirmation answer to the question whether or not he had had a hand making a certain excavation over in the river bottom. The officers conducted Dooling to the calaboose and put him behind lock and key,

there to remain until the object of the digging could be investigated.

A *News* reporter called at the calaboose. Dooling is a very black negro aged about 30 and of average colored understanding. He talked freely and gave the reporter the following account of what took place Friday night. At about 7 o'clock p.m. a man who was neither white nor black, but of a suspicious betwixt and between color, as he expressed it, called at his house, and represented to him that the spirits had told him where there was a large pile of gold buried, and that if he would accompany him and assist in unearthing it he would "divvy" with him. Being in need of a little money in his business, he without hesitation expressed his willingness to go on such an expedition. Dooling, in obedience to command, looked the place over for tools, with the result of handing a pick and an old spade. The gold hunter said that there was yet one thing lacking, and that was a Bible. Dooling was able to supply this and soon produced the Old and New Testaments and the Apocraphy complete in one volume. Thus equipped they set out, and proceeded in silence to the place where they were some time later on, discovered and surprised by Mr. Terry, who was leading Dooling in fortune stopped and took from his pocket a bright rod, numerously notched. This he held in his hand, while he pronounced voodoo incantations. Dooling could not literally interpret him, but he said the effect of his gibberish was a prayer that the spirits would show him precisely where to dig. Finally satisfying himself that he had found the proper spot, he took from his pocket four mule shoes and set them up so as to describe a square with the corners corresponding to the four cardinal points of the compass. This done, he asked Dooling to open the Bible at the Ten Commandments. Dooling readily complied, as he had the book dog-eared at that page containing the decalogue.

The open book was places on the east side of the spot selected to dig on. The mule shoes and the Bible were for the purpose of keeping evil spirits from interfering with the work. The mysterious man now went through a second series of incantations, at the conclusion of which he produced and lighted a couple of candles and told Dooling that the occult racket was for the most part at an end and that he could fall to with spade and the shovel, directing him when to dig. Dooling says he worked hard for about an hour, when his boss, who was not only attending the spirits, but also listening for any mortal prowlers that might come that way, all of a sudden "dowsed the glim" and took to his heels, commanding him to follow, which he lost no time in doing, halting not until he reached home.

Dooling having completed his narrative the reporter elicited the following additional points from him: That he did not know the man whom he accompanied on this strange expedition: that he came from Alabama to Dallas in 1878, and has since lived here: that he is a member of the African M.E. Church: that he firmly believes that spirits appear to people: that certain peculiarly favored colored people have the power to conjure others, in proof of which he showed the reporter several ugly scars on his breast, which were the result of wounds inflicted on him when

young by an Alabama conjurer: that he had every confidence that if the police would let him out he could, with the aid of the pointers he got from his director last night, soon unearth the treasures: that he both saw and heard the spirits while his companion was talking to them Friday night, and that they made a noise like unto that of cows when they smell blood, and finally that the ideas entertained by him concerning spirits, ghosts and conjuring were common to nearly all colored people.

The officers endeavored all day yesterday to find Dooling's mysterious companion, but to no effect. It was at the time reported that he had been seen in the forenoon digging in the excavation, and that he fled on the approach of the party who saw him.
—*Dallas Morning News*
August 15, 1886

EXTRA! EXTRA!

In Texas more land is farmed than in any other state.

Unexplained Phenomenon In Houston

HOUSTON- This morning about 12:30 o'clock citizens living in the First and Fourth Wards, North, were startled by a loud report that shook the houses and rattled window-glass in a lively manner. The report was loud enough to awaken those who had retired to slumber, and caused general alarm. Several gentlemen who were up at the time say the shock was very great, and felt like the Charleston earthquake. It is thought that it was caused from a meteoric fall. The shock was more severe in the Fourth Ward North, and citizens on Main Street, a mile from that ward, all concur in locating it over there. Diligent search and inquiry have failed to discover the cause.

—*Dallas Morning News*
July 30, 1887

❖ ❖ ❖

A Petrified Cow's Tail

WHITEWRIGHT- Pieces of petrified animals continue to be unearthed in the rock cut a few miles east of here on the Cotton Belt Railway. Yesterday a cow's tail and the skull of a dog were brought in and placed in exhibition in a drug store.

—*Dallas Morning News*
March 30, 1888

❖ ❖ ❖

A Peculiar Mound

RANDOLPH- There stands near this town a hill which is one of nature's wonders. It is a circular mound, about 20 yards in diameter at the top and about 100 yards at the bottom. It is though to be an ancient Indian graveyard, by the many things that are found there. The points of Indian arrows, the flint and many of the peculiarities of Indians are found here. A few years ago someone though that the Indians or Spaniards had buried money there and began digging, which revealed startling facts concerning it. Many are the stories told about this mound and many are the remarks, theories and ideas advanced. Among the many things found was a spear of flint, shaped as a knife, with a point equal to the point of a common knife. This was found by L.K. Patton of this place. Many shells and stones of peculiar colors and shapes are found and treasured as relics of the Indians of Texas.

—*Dallas Morning News*
December 16, 1888

❖ ❖ ❖

A Curious Tree

RICHMOND- There is to be seen a few miles from the outskirts of Richmond, a natural curiosity, the like of which is to be found nowhere else in the world. It is an enormous oak tree literally suspended in the air. It stands in the midst of a dense grove known as Bentley's wood, and is made quite a show of. The mystery of its suspension is that many hunting parties have camped beneath it during a period of many years. Their fires have gradually burned the truck away for a distance of six feet, but its large and spreading branches are so entwined in those of the trees growing closely about it that it is supported by them. Just how its huge bulk is nourished is a mystery, but that it is well nourished is evident, for it is green and flourishing.

—*Dallas Morning News*
October 11, 1890

A Curious Graveyard
In Which Is Buried Only The Amputated Legs And Fingers Of Railroad Men

DENISON- Denison has a most peculiar graveyard. In fact, it is probable that not another cemetery of the kind is to be found in the state. The burial ground is a small of land lying north and immediately adjoining the Missouri, Kansas and Texas freight depot, and is used for the interment of hands, legs, fingers and such other parts of human beings as are mashed or mutilated by the cars in such a manner as necessitates amputation. In the Missouri, Kansas and Texas yards in this city and among its hundreds of miles of track north, south and

west of the city accidents are frequently occurring, and a large number of those injured are forwarded here for medical and surgical treatment. The freight building is used for such purposes, and the vacant lot north of the platform is used as a depository for amputated substance. Two weeks ago the legs of little Johnny Wells were interred in this peculiar graveyard, and this morning the right foot of E.R. McCain found a grave at the same place.

—*Dallas Morning News*
May 3, 1891

❖ ❖ ❖

Names In The Graves Forgot
Discovery Of A Curious Graveyard Near Channing

CHANNING- A most interesting find, which may prove of historical interest, was made a day or two since by some well-diggers, three miles from Channing. On a high eminence overlooking the Rita Blauco Creek near a spring they came across a number of ancient bones, teeth, etc., protruding from an exposed lime rock bluff, where, in the distant past, doubtless some race of people had their burying ground. Evidently at the time of their interment, by whatever means, this ground was simply a soft lime substance and nearly level, or at least of a character not badly washed or exposed. To-day it presents a badly broken surface, on one side a bluff, and the whole is a hardening lime rock hill and the scattered and innumerable bones form simply an art of the rocky hill and can be seen and cut out everywhere.

There are bones small and large ribs, joint bones, teeth, of sizes which make them inexplicable by that repository of all information the oldest citizen. The petrifying condition of these bones, except where they are entirely decayed and the fact that they are in no way arranged, but in all sized pieces and scattered, precludes the thought that the could have been placed there by the Indians, unless very remotely, and the entire matter furnishes a puzzle alike to the old frontiersmen and college graduates. The fragments of teeth found are much longer apparently than those of a horse, though not so heavy or coarse.

Is it the burying place of some forgotten race? Has the mysterious mound builder been here? All *The News* correspondent can say is, that he proposes to investigate and sift this thing to the bottom if it takes all summer and send *The News* the results.
—*Dallas Morning News*
May 27, 1891

❖ ❖ ❖

That Mysterious Hole
The Mexicans Dug
At The Foot Of A Tree.
The All Absorbing Topic
At Corsicana.
Various Conjectures As To Object
Of The Diggers.
May Have Been A Grave.
Found No Bones.

CORSICANA- The hole the Mexicans dug is the exciting topic of conversation here at present. All day yesterday and to-day crowds of people of all classes, white and black, were continually coming to and going from the place where the digging was done. Nothing has developed so far to indicate what was found, if anything.

The excavation was made on or near the sidewalk or path at the root of a large oak tree, directly opposite and just north of the Collin Street Schoolhouse. *The News* correspondent visited the place again to-day and found that another excavation had been made a little further west, almost to the corner of the street that runs north and south of the school. It was under a large tree standing all alone north of the boy's path several rods from Collin Street, almost in the middle of the lot, surrounded by a barbed wire fence, but the dirt had either not been thrown out or else the hole had been refilled.

While the hole at the root of the first tree, that been left open, had been made in a straight line almost directly north and south and east thereof, the one at the foot of the last tree mentioned had been excavated directly north without any attempt at straight lines, but looking more as if the digging was done round and round indiscriminately, apparently attempting to find some hidden landmark. Then the excavation here, by pushing down a sharpened stick, did not seem to be more than two feet deep, while the one at the other tree had undoubtedly been dug to a depth of at least six feet.

Various conjectures have been made as to the find the Mexicans secured. The accepted theory seems to be that the place where the hole was left partially unfilled

was the last resting place of some prominent Mexican chieftain, and that jewels and other valuables, which the party knew of, had been buried with the body at the time of the interment. There are no traces of bones. The affair is still shrouded in the deepest mystery.

—*Dallas Morning News*
August 20, 1891

❖ ❖ ❖

Keep Vigil In A Graveyard

GEORGETOWN- Dr. Sam Houston and Cooper Sanson, esq., had a singular experience here Saturday night. The little daughter of Mr. and Mrs. Will Price of Lampasas County died at the home of her parents and the body was brought here to be interred in the family burial ground. A telegram was received here from Lampasas stating that the child died of some contagious disease, and the authorities requesting that the body should not be brought inside the corporation, it was left in the graveyard all night, and the two gentleman above named kept their lonely watch surrounded by the dead.

—*Dallas Morning News*
November 1, 1891

❖ ❖ ❖

The Wrong Man Buried
A San Antonio Corpse Incorrectly Identified.
A Costly Funeral For A Penniless Man.
The Other Fellow Alive.
Who Was The Dead Man?

SAN ANTONIO- About a month ago a stranger, apparently 35 years of age, came to this city from Mexico it is said. He took quarters at the Globe Hotel and remained there for ten days. One night he appeared at the Vienna Hotel on South Alamo Street with a valise and took a room. The people at the place thought he was intoxicated and paid no attention to his groans at midnight. The next morning he was found dead. He had in his possession some shirts and papers bearing the name of C.G. Jones, also a letter addressed to Charles Finehout. His body was held here pending instructions from relatives. As a result the body of the man was sent to Seymour, Ind., and the following special from that place shows the sensational turn of affairs that developed a little later. The dispatch says: "On July 1 there came to Western Union telegraph office here a telegram from San Antonio, Tex, signed A. R. Buchanan, addressed to Mr. Joe I. Moore saying:

"Young man found dead in bed at Vienna Hotel here this morning. Among his effects a recent letter from you addressed Charles Finehout. Other letters and wearing apparel marked C.G. Jones. Wire information.

"The attaches of the telegraph office were twenty-four hours in tracing the ownership of this message to Mrs. Josephine Isaacs

Moore, wife of one of our prominent manufacturers and daughter of C.C. Isaacs, a retired farmer. Mr. Isaacs at once replied to the message as follows:

"Think corpse my nephew, Charles Finehout. Can it be shipped here?" "He also telegraphed Mr. Francis Schuh, formerly of this city but now of San Antonio, to ascertain if the corpse at the Vienna Hotel was that of Charles Finehout.

"Charles Finehout is or was a man of about 28 years of age, tall, strong, and well built, who spent nearly all of his early life here, but who for the past six years had been in the southwest holding positions on different railroads as fireman and engineer. When home on a visit a year ago he admitted that he traveled under an assumed name, Frank Melville, the greater part of the time. When last heard from six weeks ago, he was at Santa Rosalia, Mexico, where he said he was an engineer on the Mexican Central Railroad and that he was in good health, had saved up $500 and intended to make a visit home shortly, but not until after he had gone to the City of Mexico to join the Brotherhood of Locomotive Engineers.

"In due course answers to Mr. Isaacs' telegraph were received, the one from Schuh saying, 'Corpse at Vienna is that of Charles Finehout.' And from Buchanan. 'Body can be shipped, but not in presentable condition.' Isaacs went immediately to the First National Bank and had them telegraph Buchanan to ship the remains here and guaranteeing the charges. On July 6 the box was received here with advanced and express charges of $187. This was paid and the remains taken to the home of Mr. Isaacs on North Walnut Street. There the box was opened and the coffin exposed to view. It was of the very cheapest kind, probably costing about $20.

"It was opened and it was found that it was not lined and that the remains were packed in sawdust. The face was uncovered and although decomposition was well advanced, some of the friends who were present declared that the remains were not those of Charles Finehout. However, there was nothing done, and the coffin was closed and religious ceremonies held, and the remains were interred in a new lot, just purchased by Mr. Isaacs in River View Cemetery.

"After the funeral ceremonies were concluded an examination was made of the contents of the valise. Aside from the Joe I. Moore letter and one or two photographs there was nothing in the valise to indicate that it was the property of Charles Finehout. Other articles in the valise were shirts marked C.G. Jones, letters and documents addressed to the same name. Among the latter was a certificate from the general office of the Mexican Central Railroad to the effect that C.G. Jones was traveling auditor for that company. This of course, served to arouse the suspicions of the relatives that they had buried the remains of some other than Charles Finehout, and they immediately sought to get word to him at Santa Rosalia, where last heard from. No answers came, however to their telegrams, and they concluded that they had made no mistake and that Charles Finehout was dead and buried. They decided to trace Jones, and sent a number of letters, detailing the circumstances, addressed to the correspondents of Jones, as found in the valise.

"On yesterday their suspicions that Finehout was not dead were confirmed when by the receipt of a letter from him dated Las Vegas, N.M., July 1 and postmarked July 4, saying he was well and hearty. Telegrams since exchanged are conclusive evidence that he is alive and well, and will be in Seymour within a few days.

"But who is the man sleeping his last sleep up there in the beautiful $200 lot in River View? Who is C.G. Jones? Where is he? Is he dead; or was the man a thief who stole from both Finehout and Jones? Who is to reimburse Isaacs in the expense incident to the burial of the unknown, nearly $400? Since Finehout's last visit here his grandfather had died, leaving him property valued at $10,000."

—*Dallas Morning News*
July 25, 1892

Prehistoric Ruins In Texas
Twenty Miles Of Solid Masonry Resembling The Chinese Wall

MILANO- A Texas correspondent writes to one of the scientific departments of the government of a strangely interesting prehistoric wall discovered on the frontier of the Lone Star state. This marvelous ruin surpasses in interest all the other wonderful remains hitherto found of the people who once inhabited the whole Mexican plateau and attained a high state of civilization. It passes through Milano and has a total length of about twenty miles. It is built of solid masonry ten to fifteen feet high and as many feet thick.

Its height and thickness are thus almost as great as the famous Chinese wall on the north of China. The direction is northeast and southwest. It is the most part underground and this is one of the curious things that puzzle those wise men who are supposed to know all about prehistoric remains. It is undoubtedly very old. One might suppose it to be the sure foundation of a gigantic fortress which rose above the ground many feet.

The tower and other means of defense with which it might have been provided have had time to crumble away in the years that have passed. The long fortress may have been pulled down by the conquering invaders. As the people died out from the land, the debris of the old wall would in either case cover its foundation.

The Aztecs probably built this wall. They

have left some inscriptions upon it, but since their language is entirely lost no scholar can ever hope to decipher them. One covers a space of eight feet square. The characters are kindred to Indian inscriptions, but not so closely allied that their mystery can be penetrated. There was undoubtedly a populous village or city in the vicinity, for on a high hill the remains of a mighty temple of worship are found. This was supported by more than 200 lofty pillars.

Some of them are still standing. They were made of clay, which was well burned. This gave them the appearance of stone. In this temple were placed many idols, broken parts of which are preserved. One shaped like an owl is preserved entire. Human sacrifices were made to these, as well as sacrifices of birds, beasts and reptiles. Skulls and bones have been preserved in the clay. Some of these belonged to very large animals.

Some are petrified, and it is thought that those early Aztecs may have understood the art of petrifaction and thus preserved the bones of their sacrifices. The idols are all curiously marked. Around each pillar small stones are piled up in circles or squares, and inside each circle, underneath the pillar, there is a center of foundation stone, fashioned to represent the godhead. Near the wall there are also furnaces in which the natives smelted iron.

The locality and direction of the wall are not easily accounted for. Perhaps it marks the boundary of certain tribal territory which was exposed to the attacks of the enemy. An enormous amount of labor and material must have been required for its construction if built above the ground on the same gigantic plan as the foundation. Although there were toward 1,000,000 people then living in that vicinity, the work must have extended over a considerable amount of time.

Unless it was some straight point it is difficult to understand how but a few thousands could be interested in the construction. An old tradition says that the Aztecs were one of the seven powerful tribes that emerged from the seven caverns in a region called Azlion, or place of the heron. They wandered away from their fellows after a great confusion of tongues and settled in the region they are known to have inhabited. This tradition may be partly fabulous, but it is sure that the Aztecs settled the country before the eleventh or twelfth century.

All the tribes lived in peace for a considerable time, until the strong began to encroach upon the territory of the weak. Then a fierce war for supremacy of the whole territory ensued and lasted many years. Under the leadership of their military chiefs the Aztecs obtained control of the territory and established a very enlightened form of government. This was consummated in 1324 or 1325. It is likely that the fortress was built during this period of war.

—*Dallas Morning News*
May 22, 1893

Legends Of The Hills
**History And Romance Of The
Mountains Above Austin.
A Story Of Lee's Fight
With The Indians.
Loyal To The Old Flag.
Beauty Of The Lake Scenery.**

AUSTIN- It is a wild, ragged, mountainous region on either side of the dam lake a distance of twenty-five miles and even up to and above Marble Falls, extending from the lake shores from two to ten miles out. These Colorado hills abound in rock. They are separated by canyons, some of which are highly picturesque. Whenever there is soil mountain cedar, live oak and other evergreens grow.

Upon three acres of mountain side belonging to the Chatauqua grounds there are over thirty varieties of tree growth, presenting every phase of foliage and every shade of green. Along the stony declivities near the water edge great varieties of ferns of luxuriant growth are found, but the spoiler from the city is fast thinning them out. Wild grapes and all kinds of vines abound along the water's edge, in the

canyons and wherever a plat of ground affords life-hold for plant growth. A vast region through which the Colorado winds above the city, where it debouches into the plains, is of this description.

Mountainous hills, great boulders fallen to the little valleys, precipitous mountain sides where upon the stone ledges and in the crevices of rock a little soil has been gathered or has been left in which trees, vines, shrubs, ferns and flowers grow in profusion; caves, springs of sparkling cool water and birds, squirrels and rabbits, and out in the wilder and more inaccessible places deer hiding out by day all invite the idle city lounger to ascend the lake and explore the wilderness.

Most visitors and Austin people are content to view the scenery from the deck or the Ben Hur or some lesser lake steamer upon the delusive fancy that only "Tis distance lends enchantment to the view," and that nearer are merely uninviting details of time-worn and broken rock and scanty wood growth. A few however, camp upon the lake side far up in the hills, and are delighted with the closer inspection of the fantastics in vegetable, herb, and mineral growth. The atmosphere is purity itself and many degrees cooler than in the town; there are no mosquitoes or flies; fish are plenty and easily caught when city worms are to be had; the birds warble, and the camper, after a few days of rambling, sleeps soundly and eats like a tramp.

Through the mountains—as we call them—wherever there is a valley of ten to thirty acres of land level enough for the cultivation is found the actual settler. The land is usually very productive. The mountaineer is able to raise enough corn and garden truck for his use, and until the dam lake submerged the river road hauled wood to Austin, often a distance of twenty miles, for money to buy calico, coffee, ammunition, tobacco and snuff. On some few river farms enough land was found before the lake invaded the fields to raise all the crops.

Back away from the river in these hills there are few living. The denizens generally are a hardy people, but they are shrewd and unexpectedly well informed, though disposed to be unsuspicious and too credulous. They are, with rare exceptions, of the same families that occupied this region before the confederate war. As one of the old grizzled ones said to me on the deck of the Ben Hur, whispering and looking around suspiciously to see if the conscript officer was near, "We was all for the old flag."

I found the old gentleman knew the mountain history from the time the Comanches rendezvoused there when they raided around Austin killing settlers and driving off stock, and when that region later was visited by the advance agents of the fleeing Mormons and a Mormon settlement was established on the river below and above the mouth of Bull Creek, a few miles above the dam, when later it became the refuge of Texas unionists evading and fighting confederate conscript officers and down to this day of the dam when he travels to the city on the deck of a large steamboat.

From him I learned that the mountain peo-ple here as in Tennessee, Kentucky, West Virginia and other mountain districts of the southern states sided with the "old flag." They did not propose to fight their neighbors of the plains and were content to stay at home and take no pay in the war. They almost worshiped Jack Hamilton, who was compelled to take refuge in their midst. The old man told me about a speech Hamilton made to them when the home guards, led by conscript officers, were hunting them down. It was in a wild part of the country which he pointed out. Hamilton, mounted on a huge rock, spoke earnestly against the proposition of some of the younger men to organize.

A guerrilla warfare against the confederate conscript officers. He eloquently opposed the cruel warfare between neighbors of the hills and plains, and urged those who desired to fight to leave and join the regular union forces. Some few followed the advice, making their way, as did Hamilton, John Hancock and others, through the confederate lines and joined the federal army. One at least of them is now drawing a pension from Uncle Sam.

A leading man among them together with a small following, however, became fugitives, hiding in the hills and secluded valleys and working their little crops as occasion permitted. Some few joined the home guards but never expected to fight against the "old flag." A hardy and shrewd mountaineer made frequent trips between these hills and the federal army, it was presumed giving intelligence of what was transpiring about the state capital.

The old pioneer who related these things

pointed out a place below San Monica Springs where one of the fugitives from the conscript officers, who were in close pursuit, jumped off a precipice sheer fifty feet to the rocks below and was so disabled that he was captured. Below this point a short distance is a small level valley, at the foot of the Chautauqua hill which was pointed out as the place where Robert E. Lee, in command of regulars, had a fight with a raiding band of Comanches, killing half the marauders. The legend is questioned, because the oldest inhabitant knows nothing of the fight. It is true the Comanches used to cross the river at that point, coming up the little canyon and striking directly for the rapids just above the dam, cutting off two bands in the river and reaching the vicinity of Austin around the foot of Mount Bonnel, but if Lee ever fought them below Burnet no one ever heard of it or spoke of it about here until the dam revived interest in the history of these rugged hills. Some romance has probably transferred the scene of one of Lee's battles with the redskins so as to fit in with the projects of his friends, the suburban town lot boomers.

I asked the old mountaineer if there was any fighting and killing in the hills during the late war, and he said that further up the river above the head of the lake, in the wildest district, it is believed many were killed, but he could never learn the names. It was currently reported in the troubled times that a number of fugitives who made fight were fusilladed. The writer many years ago heard such a report to the effect that a good many union men had been murdered in these mountains, but inquiry then, as now, failed to disclose the partici-

pants and the victims. At any rate, it would be a great country for partisan fighting.

It is well worth a trip to Austin to take a boat and ascend this stream to the head of the lake, and, time permitting, to camp out, explore the fastnesses and gather fossils and ferns. The visitors will find something novel and beautiful on all sides, not the least being the extensive inland lake of clear, pure water, mirroring the wild and precipitous mountain sides and luxurious vegetation upon the level slopes.

—*Dallas Morning News*
June 27, 1893

❖ ❖ ❖

Found Treasure

WHARTON- Some little boys plowing on the river banks near town Thursday evening discovered several pieces of coin. They began digging with their hands and were repeatedly rewarded with success until an amount approximating $70 was secured. How the money came buried there is a mystery.

—*Dallas Morning News*
August 21, 1893

❖ ❖ ❖

A Strange Coin

The Search For Gold Coin Buried By Santa Fe Traders

WACO- The following dated Navasota, May 12 has been going the rounds of the press:

"A party has been organized here to seek for a great quantity of gold said to have been sunk some sixty years ago in a slough about twenty miles above here by a party of Santa Fe traders, who were hard pressed by a band of Indians and to save their lives were forced to get rid of the large quantity of coin which they had tied to buckskins on the backs of burros."

The forgoing gives rise to some interesting conjectures, and to some romantically inclined perhaps a wild dream as gorgeous as that which led De Soto to roam the wilderness and find a grave at last in the Mississippi.

There is probably some truth in this legendary deposit of gold. There is scarcely a community in Texas, from the Red River to the Colorado, that has not lingering around it in the memory of the old settlers and in the imagination of the young some thread of the tangled skein of that old legend. Many a man in the dead of night has crept into his neighbor's field or pasture and delved into the soil for that which he never found. Many of man, when he should have been pulling the bell-cord of a pair of amiable pair of mules, had spent his valuable time in stalking over the ground with a divining rod while the cockleburs and sunflowers encroached upon his corn. And many a fellow who would find it a gruesome toil to wield the festive hoe in the crabgrass has disregarded his constitutional proclivities and heaved ton after ton of dirt out of some hole and thereby benefited his muscle and not his pocket. Many an idle enthusiast guiltless of a bath at all other times has overcome his aversion to water and waded some creek, prying into

nooks and crannies for the "broad pieces of yellow gold" left there by some flying Don Alfonso who was pursued by some noble Geronimo.

The writer of these lines has in his possession a coin that had caused many a weed to flourish in the cotton field and many a gap in the pasture fences to go unattended. It has caused the virgin sod to be invaded by pick and shovel. It has caused large, clear blisters on hands that never knew blisters before. It has caused more than one man to get his legs tangled up with the long handle of a spade in the wild effort to manipulate said spade in a six-foot hole. It has caused the suspicious soul of some peaceable citizen to be shocked with the spectacle of a new made grave in his peach orchard, with all the accompanying horrors of robbery and murder. And so far as this writer knows no distorted body has been found beneath that dirt, and no mate of this strange coin had ever turned it broad face to the morning sun.

It is a gold coin, worth about $18. On one side is stamped "Rebublica de Colombia," and is dated 1832. On the crown of the goddess of liberty is inscribed "Bogota" and "8 S.R.S." surrounding a cornucopia, with a battle-ax, bow, arrow and quiver. It is not perfectly round, and the mintage is crude. But it is that peculiar yellow gold which comes from South America. The coin was bored out of the ground with a post auger by a gentleman in the county near the old fortifications and breastworks near West, said to have been made by the Spanish traders some time between 1832 and 1840, when the final battle was fought with Indians. The coin was about a foot

under the surface. Many searches have been made, by no other money has been found.

—*Dallas Morning News*
May 20, 1894

❖ ❖ ❖

An Odd Coincidence

HILLSBORO- John Gentry, colored, who was stabbed in an affray here on the night of the 22nd, died last night. His dying statement was that a certain Hillsboro darky stabbed him. His death recalls an oft-repeated saying that somebody is killed during the sitting of every grand jury in Hill County. The record shows such to have been the case back to the killing of Jonas Land in 1885. Whether the sitting of the grand jury stirs up men's evil passions to the slaying point or whether the slaying during its sittings is a coincidence is left for the curious.

—*Dallas Morning News*
March 29, 1895

❖ ❖ ❖

Well Preserved Coffin

WAXAHACHIE- While workmen were engaged in tearing away an old blacksmith shop Saturday a metallic coffin was unearthed. It was in a perfect state of preservation and when opened the cushions and linings looked as fresh as they did twenty-six years ago. The coffin originally belonged to Capt. J.B. Meredith, who dealt in coffins in 1869. It was the only one he had left and he put it in the black-smith shop for safe keeping.

—*Dallas Morning News*
July 16, 1895

❖ ❖ ❖

Buried In The Same Coffin

TERRELL- May and Oma. The little 3 and 6-year-old daughters of D.H. Myers died yesterday but a few hours apart, of sporadic diphtheria. They were buried in the same coffin.

—*Dallas Morning News*
November 24, 1895

❖ ❖ ❖

A Peculiar Coincidence

SHERMAN- To-day at the union passenger station the subject of coincidences was the topic, and Allen Blake, ex-tax assessor, but now in charge of the transfer of mail from non-terminal trains, remarked that May 26 had been the date of several of the most important events in his life. Continuing in explanation he said:

"I was born May 26, 1832, twenty-five years later on May 26, 1857, I was married: four years later, on May 26, 1861, I enlisted in the confederate army and on May 26, 1865 I got back home. So you can understand I am always prepared to see some unusual event occur to me on that day."

—*Dallas Morning News*
December 29, 1896

Strange Coincidence

LONGVIEW- In the district court yesterday there were two trials for wife murder bearing so close a resemblance to each other as to be curious and excite remark. Both defendants were negroes and each claimed the killing was accidental. Both were tried the same day, convicted and sentenced to prison for life, and each one is named Williams. Judge, juries, spectators and witnesses seemed to be confused over the two cases so similar.

—*Dallas Morning News*
December 31, 1896

Hidden Treasure In A Lake
A Story Of Gold
Under The water Of Lake Onstott

BONHAM- Nine miles northwest from this city lies a beautiful sheet of water called Onstott's Lake. A dense growth of huge forest trees extends some distance around. It is a lovely place, and has for some years past become a popular resort for picnics and other public gatherings on account of the shade and abundance of pure water.

From early days there has been a legend among the residents adjacent to the lake that there was hidden beneath its placid waters or somewhere thereabouts a vast treasure of some kind. Of what it consisted none knew. The story was vague and indefinite. Yet the early settlers have often told that there was untold wealth hidden somewhere about the lake.

The News Reporter has heard this report before now and passed it unnoticed, deeming it idle talk and forgetting it soon after hearing it. But yesterday the story was vividly brought to the mind of the reporter and revived the story about Onstott's Lake. About 1 o'clock yesterday evening an old man, seeming 70 years of age, came into the city and spent a couple of hours, and in making some inquiries he causally stated that he was on his way to Onstott's Lake; that he was going there in search of buried treasure, hearing which *The News* reporter engaged the old man in conversation, and in answer to questions he said his name was M. Austin, and that he had just arrived from west Texas; that in 1868 he joined a colony of Americans in St. Louis and went to Venezuela, South America. He said when they arrived there the government gave to each colonist 1280 acres in order to encourage immigration: that some of this land was agricultural and some mineral. This was done to encourage both agricultural and mining interests and develop the resources of the country. While most of the colonists resorted to mining, he being much impressed with the character of the soil, determined to engage in agricultural pursuits, and having no plow, he hunted up an old piece of iron which they had brought among their effects. He went to work and made him a plow, the first ever made in Venezuela. He secured a native with a yoke of oxen, and hitching them to his plow, the yoke being fastened to horns of the cattle in front of their heads instead of being on their necks like we work oxen here, and soon he had four acres plowed, the first land ever plowed in Venezuela.

The only seed he had were two ears of corn, one white and the other yellow, and a few vegetable seeds. These he planted and his crop came up and thrived. The yellow corn matured in six weeks, but the white corn, although it grew large, did not bear any fruit. The vegetables yielded abundantly.

There were 180 colonists and they settled near the city of Bolivar, not a great distance from the mouth of the Orinoco river. He remained there two years. Most of the colonists turned their attention to mining, and finding that they did not realize much from that source and the climate being so unhealthy most of them sickened and died the first year, and those who survived escaped from the country the first opportunity offered.

After two years he became tired and not being able to stand the climate also determined to leave. The president of Venezuela sent for him and tried to induce him to stay, but he feared the climate and left the country and made his way to Mexico about the first of the year 1870. While prospecting in that country an American was arrested, tried and convicted on a charge of murder and was sentenced to the penitentiary for life. He had met him up in the mining districts and had

become well acquainted with him, and before he was transported to the penitentiary he sent for the visitor, and said to me that way back during the Texas Revolution he belonged to a band of robbers: that they piled their avocation principally in Texas, making raids on the principal towns and robbing the banks: that they committed several robberies in the city of Jefferson, and had accumulated a vast amount of gold and silver coin: that they were making their way out of the country to evade the officers who were after them: that they stopped and camped on Onstott's Lake to rest their horses.

While camped there a body of Mexican soldiers discovered and attacked them. A fierce battle was fought, during which all of the robbers were killed except himself: that he alone escaped: that during the battle their treasure was thrown in Onstott's Lake to preserve it from being captured by the Mexicans: that he escaped to Mexico, and now that he was sentenced to the penitentiary for life he would be unable to go back to the lake and secure the treasure they had thrown in the water to prevent it from falling into the hands of the Mexican soldiers. He then detailed the exact locality in the lake where it was thrown. He said it was a vast amount and considered of gold and silver coin placed in stout buckskin bags, and that he had never revealed the whereabouts of the treasure. He said he hoped that Austin would be lucky enough to secure the treasure and enjoy it. Austin thanked the man for the information and told him that he would go in search of it as soon as he could make arrangements.

It was seven years before Austin could

come to Texas and visit Onstott's Lake, which he did about two years ago. It was in the summer time and Austin told Mr. Pierce, who lives near the lake, about the treasure and wanted him and his boys to stop work and go with him in search of the money, but he could not quit his crops at that time of the year, so after a visit to the lake Austin located the spot where the treasure was buried from the description given him by his friend in Mexico. Austin then left for west Texas and has been out there ever since prospecting for mineral, but now Austin is on his way to Onstott's Lake after that money and says he is going to secure it. He has in his possession a mineral rod which will show him, he says, the exact spot in the lake where the money lies. Saying which the old man said he must go, as he wished to reach his point of destination before night.

—*Dallas Morning News*
January 22, 1897

❖ ❖ ❖

A Peculiar Excavation

SHERMAN- Health Officer Charles May examined a peculiar excavation in Springdale suburb this evening and found where a camp had been pitched last night. A bois d'arc post, the end of which had been buried at least two feet out of sight, had been located and taken out. To all appearances it had been there many years and marked some spot. Who the campers were and what they wanted is still a mystery.

—*Dallas Morning News*
August 21, 1897

EXTRA! EXTRA!

Historians also believe that during 1861, several members of the Texas Volunteers died from measles and pneumonia, while camped near Onstott's Lake.

Hidden Treasure Rumors

DENTON- Since the report in *The News* of buried treasure being found a few miles west of here, other rumors of large amounts of hidden silver have been going the rounds. One report, or rumor, is that several miles west of Aubrey, just opposite the mouth of Cedar Creek, a large sum of money in silver bullion was hidden by the Mexicans long before the coming of the white man into this part of the state. It is also said that several years ago an old Mexican, in a covered wagon, came into that vicinity in which the bullion is supposed to have been secreted, and by the aid of a chart attempted to locate it, with what success, however, has never been known, as the old fortune-hunter was very reticent about his actions, and nothing whatever could be learned from that source. At any rate, it was known that he dug into the ground many times at many places, and many believed that he located the bullion and took it away with him. But there were fully as many who thought this part of the story unfounded, and still believe in the existence of the hidden treasure, and every now and then indulge in fitful efforts to locate it.

So far, however, if success has ever attended the search, it has never been definitely known, and the treasure, if such there be, has lain for years, and will lie peacefully for as many more, unless some believer in the old legend, more fortunate than any of his predecessors, by some lucky stumble, accidentally strikes the rich find, tells it, it is published in *The News*, and there will be another generation of fools to once more begin the search for other hidden fortunes.

—*Dallas Morning News*
January 17, 1899

❖ ❖ ❖

Old Graves Found
Supposed To Be Of Parties Caught By Owls During The War

SHERMAN- A young farmer by the name of Pate, who lives about four miles east of the city, in clearing up some undergrowth, found several graves. He dug down into one of them until he came to a box, and there he desisted. The oldest citizen of that section does not remember of a burial taking place at the point where the graves were found.

There is a story that during the war an old man, his two sons, and a couple of desperate characters with them, escaped the conscription officers of the struggling confederacy, remaining in the bushes and stealing the stock left at home in the possession of the women and the faithful slaves. Their depredation were not confined exclusively to the vicinity of Sherman but their headquarters were in an hour's ride of the courthouse. One day a squad of confederate soldiers captured them in Sherman and started out to Bonham with them. A few miles out, and near the graves that were found by Pate, a party of civilians, old men and small boys met the soldiers and assisted the prisoners to escape, and the story goes still further to the effect that so eager were the civilians to keep the clutches of the soldiers off them that they strung them up to pecan trees, out of reach of even a bayonet. They were cut down the next day and buried. They are probably the occupants of the graves discovered by Pate.

—*Dallas Morning News*
January 19, 1889

❖ ❖ ❖

Unearthed A Graveyard

WACO- A force of graders working under the direction of Capt. Stephen Turner, the city engineer, while cutting through a hill to bring North Eighth Street to a better level opened an ancient cemetery which contains relics which some people regard as being the work of the mound builders. Most of the specimens are stone. There are weapons of war and the chase, beads and the tools of prehistoric artisans. The curiosities were appropriated by people who collected rapidly at the scene of the find. The city engineer collected a portion of the relics and turned them over to Baylor University. The truck of a mastodon was found among the human bones and other antiquities. One article discovered in the pit is a curved piece of metal encrusted with pebbles, clay and shells, having the appearance of a sword blade. About a bushel of flint spear and arrow heads was dug out of the hill.

For twenty years or more excavators here-abouts have been making discoveries of bones of prehistoric animals, gigantic human bones, and all sorts of weapons and tools. City Engineer Turner thinks a grand discovery will yet be made in digging around Waco, which will startle the scientists of the world.

—*Dallas Morning News*
January 24, 1899

❖ ❖ ❖

Ruins Of An Ancient City In Texas

SOCORRO- The surveys at present being made for the Kansas City, El Paso and Mexican railroad company at a point north latitude 33° and west longitude 106°, have passed along the lave flow which by the local population is called the Molpais. It consists of a sea of molten black glass, agitated at the moment of cooling in ragged waves of fantastic shapes. These lave waves or ridges are from ten to twelve feet high, with combing crests. This lave flow is about forty miles long from northeast to southwest, and from one to ten miles wide. For miles on both sides the country is the most desolate that can be imagined. It has been literally burnt up. It consists of fine white ashes to any depth which, so far, has been dug down.

To the north of the lava flow, and lying in the country equally desolate and arid, the surveyors have come upon the ruins of Gran Guivera, known already to the early Spanish explorers, by which have been visited by white men less often even than the mysterious ruins of Palenqus, in Central America. Only a few people at Socorro and White Oaks have been at Gran Guivera, because it is at present forty miles from water. The surveyors found the ruins to be of gigantic stone buildings made in the most substantial manner and of grand proportions. One of them was four acres in extent.

All indication around the ruins point to the existence here at one time of a dense population. No legend of any kind exists as to how the great city was destroyed or when it was abandoned. One of the engineers attached to the surveying expedition advances the theory that Gran Guivera was in existence and abundantly supplied with water at the time the terrible volcanic eruption took place.

—*Dallas Morning News*
February 23, 1889

An Indian Mound
Some Boys Dig Into It, Finding Various Trinkets And A Skeleton.

CISCO- Last Sunday, while some boys were strolling about on Mr. Sublet's place near Dehmas' tank, they came across a mound, and determined to dig into it, to see what they could find. It turned out to be an Indian grave. They found a skeleton, a gun, beads and trinkets in great numbers. Several Mexican dollars were also found in the grave. Among the trinkets were bracelets, rings, etc., carved in the most expert manner. The find was a most unexpected and gratifying one. The trinkets were brought to town and exhibited on the streets of Cisco yesterday.

—*Dallas Morning News*
March 14, 1889

❖ ❖ ❖

Hydrophobia

GREENVILLE- From Quinian there comes the report of one of the saddest and most pitiful cases of physical suffering ever recorded in Hunt County. Seven years ago, W. K. Steger and Holland Pitts were bitten by a mad dog. One year after Pitts died from hydrophobia, but Stegar never at any time showed any symptoms of the dread malady. Six weeks ago he was bitten by a cat, and last Friday when he came from work he told his wife he was sick. His condition continued to grow worse until Saturday, when he lost his mind and attacked his wife. Neighbors were notified and came in and overpowered the unfortunate victim and physicians pronounced the malady hydrophobia. It requires the effort of five or six men to hold him in bed, and he is being attended by Dr. Yates of Poetry and Dr. Merchant of Quinian. When neighbors and friends come in and offer to shake hands, the sufferer has to be watched closely and held or he will bite them. The afflicted man is the son of "Squire Stegar," a well known citizen of Quinian.

—*Rockdale Messenger*
June 8, 1899

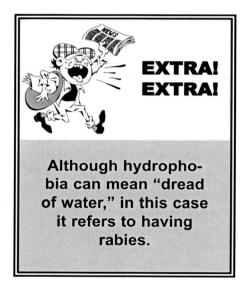

EXTRA! EXTRA!

Although hydrophobia can mean "dread of water," in this case it refers to having rabies.

Accident

NACOGDOCHES- A young man named Poland accidentally shot himself in the side with a pistol at the home of August Dewitz near Nacogdoches, from which he died in a few hours. He was visiting his sweetheart at the time and was playing with the pistol as if to shoot himself in her presence, when he let it go off.

—*Rockdale Messenger*
June 22, 1899

their own tribes. The son who traveled toward the setting sun was Nacogdoches.

Prehistoric Man
Part Of Such A Man Was Found Below The Surface

PORT LAVACA- A discovery was made here this week that will be of interest to scientific men over the state. While putting down a well at the home of Dr. C.T. Scott, human remains were found at a depth of twenty-seven feet below the surface. Parts of the skull bone of what was evidently a powerful man give an indication of the kind of people buried there, and serves to confirm the belief that the remains are of a prehistoric race and were deposited there ages ago when the coast country was in a formative state and was the habitat of huge beasts and birds that have long since disappeared from the earth. Part of the skull bone kept on exhibition at the doctor's office is petrified. The digging has not been extensive enough to determine whether or not there was an ancient graveyard on the spot.

—*Dallas Morning News*
August 14, 1899

❖ ❖ ❖

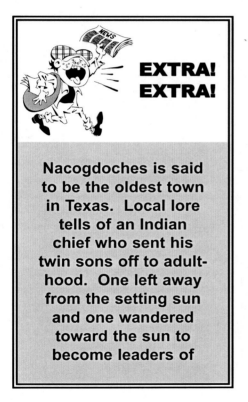

EXTRA! EXTRA!

Nacogdoches is said to be the oldest town in Texas. Local lore tells of an Indian chief who sent his twin sons off to adulthood. One left away from the setting sun and one wandered toward the sun to become leaders of

Weird Texas Romance
A Crime So Repugnant
That It Withered The Leaves And
Surrounding Vegetation.
She Miraculously Saved Her
Lover's Life And Could Live No
Longer When He Was
At Last Done To Death.

MCKINNEY- The writer noticed in *The News* of several weeks ago a story with a romantic tinge, written by Mr. Wheliss, in which he spoke of "Mormon Grove," in Grayson County, Tex., how it got the name, and of a romantic occurrence which transpired there some years ago.

Having had the pleasure of spending a night in that historic place, and meeting and being acquainted with several of the early pioneers of the community in which Mormon Grove is located, and having heard queer stories connected with the place, I will relate one that, while there are evidences at the present time to confirm part of it, sounds somewhat out of the usual order of things. Yet it is told by the old-timers of that vicinity, and in such a manner as to impress the listener that at least the teller of the story believes it to be true in the most minute detail.

In the midst, near the center of a clump of tress and standing at a considerable distance from any tree or any vegetation of any description, stands a massive tree of the forest oak variety, on which no leaf or bud has been seen for twenty-two years, so the legend goes, and the bottom—the portion next to the ground—of which seems to be petrified; and connected with this tree there is a story, which for romance and for

a display of woman's deep love and devotion, seems without a parallel, and which shows the seeming heartlessness sometimes displayed by the "vigilance committees" that existed in the early days of Texas, as well as neighboring states. The tree referred to stands in the southwestern portion of Mormon Grove.

To get at the beginning of the affair it will be necessary to go back a short time previous to the eventful days at Mormon Grove. About twenty-three years ago, and some time after the Mormons had made an invasion into Texas, a good deal of depredation had been done by Indians in north Texas and southwestern Arkansas. It was suspected that Fred Brownlee, a young man considered pretty tough, and who was raised near Ultima Thules, Howard County, Ark., was at the head of a band of roving Apaches who were going about plundering. This suspicion became so strong that a called meeting of the "regulators" was held and it was at once decided, so it is said to make short work of young Brownlee at the first opportunity. At any rate one sunny morning in May, in 1865, the house of Robert F. Brownlee, a respectable settler and farmer and father of the young man spoken of, was surrounded by a crowd of men to the number of about twenty-five who demanded the unconditional surrender of the son, Fred Brownlee. The old man, appearing at the door, informed them that Fred would join them shortly, as he had just awakened from a night's slumber and was then dressing. After waiting for some five or ten minutes the "committee" grew impatient and proceeded to enter the house, whereupon it was discovered that young Brownlee had in some manner escaped. A hurried examination of the premises showed that he had gone via the stable and had possessed himself of a horse. It did not take them long to strike the trail, however, and then began the race for life. Fred Brownlee realized that his life was at stake and rode as he had never ridden before.

A few miles from the Brownlee farm, and perhaps adjoining it, was another farmhouse in which the Wilson family resided, and the most interesting member of which was a fair-haired, blue-eyed maiden of nineteen summers. And it seems that she was not different from many other of her sex, inasmuch as she had met her fate—had fallen in love with a man, and that man was no other than Fred Brownlee, the man who was now being pursued by a band of determined men for his life.

Upon hearing of the danger that her lover had been subjected to she at once resolved to follow the pursuing band and render him any aid within her power, and even more to give up her life in his behalf if necessary, and despite the objections of parents she saddled a horse and procuring firearms started after the pursued and the pursuers. From Ultima Thules young Brownlee took a southwesterly course and reached the Indian territory, when he was captured near where Armstrong Academy now stands. He was given a few minutes to confess and make arrangements to cross the dark river. He stood firm to the last, denying that he was in any way implicated as charged and declaring his innocence. All the declarations and pleadings were in vain, however, and he was soon ornamenting a tree in the vicinity, dangling at the end of a rope.

After hanging him the regulators rode away, apparently satisfied that they had done their duty. They had no more got out of sight when Sarah Wilson (for this was the young lady's name, who had ridden all this distance in the hope of rendering her lover some aid), appeared and in a few minutes had Brownlee down—before his life was extinct—and after working with him for a short while, succeeded in fully restoring him.

After his miraculous escape from death, Brownlee, together with his fair rescuer, started for the Texas border, both riding the same horse, the one which had been ridden from Arkansas by Miss Wilson. Taking the old stage road at a point south of where he came so near meeting his death, they pursued it until they came within a short distance of where Colbert Station now is, where they stopped for rest, and which stop proved fatal for both of them, for several of the vigilance committee had also concluded to come over into Texas and spied them.

Another chase here began, and for the second time Brownlee was being pursued. And this time not alone. They finally crossed over into Texas, crossing the Red River at the north of Sherman, and passing that city to its west, arrived at Mormon Grove, and being hotly pursued, determined to stay in the friendly brush covering that portion of the country, where they hoped to conceal themselves until nightfall, having reached there during the forenoon. The regulators came upon them about noon, capturing them. Brownlee asked that his life be spared, again declaring that he was an innocent man, and promising to never again enter Arkansas. Sarah Wilson, the girl who had dared so much for the sake of the love she bore for this man, pleaded with them to spare him, but all to no avail, and he was again hanged, and on the tall oak tree spoken of in the beginning of this narrative, and this time his body was shot full of lead, thus making sure of the work. For Sarah Wilson there was nothing left to do. Her mission in life was seemingly filled. She had loved like other people perhaps, but had her love put to a test seldom experienced by a human being and now that the object of that love had been cruelly torn from her just at the time when she had dared to hope that she would receive a reward for the devotion she had shown, was more than she could bear and giving a piteous moan, she sank to the ground, never to rise again.

The next day her body, and also the body of Fred Brownlee, was found and side by side they were buried under the tree in which Brownlee had been hanged. The tree died with the summer, and is known as the "haunted tree." It is also said that not a bird or living thing had ever been known to alight in its branches since, and for a space of several feet around it the earth has effused to yield vegetables of any kind. I have often heard vague reports concerning this particular occurrence at Mormon Grove, but recently met a young man in that vicinity, who made me acquainted with the facts, and they may be deemed upon as authentic.

—*Dallas Morning News*
September 29, 1889

Remarkable Coincidence

WACO- All the sixteen jurors impaneled for the week, commencing to-morrow, have surnames commencing with the letter B. Sheriff Baker discovered this fact this morning and said he had never heard of such an incident before. The men had been selected at random by the jury commissioners.

—*Dallas Morning News*
October 2, 1899

Hays County Phenomenon

AUSTIN- A remarkable and unexplained phenomenon is reported from Hays County. During the protracted drought which prevailed throughout this section about two months ago, the dry fork of the San Marcos River became filled with a stream of clear, pure water. The creek had been dry for many years, and it is a mystery where the water came from. There has been no decrease in the flow and it seems to be of a permanent nature. Wells in that section which had been dry for many years and abandoned were also filled with water, and the supply seems to be inexhaustible. It is the theory of some that this water supply comes from Lake McDonald through an underground channel in the limestone rocks and is the cause of the rapid depletion of water in the lake.

—*Dallas Morning News*
November 28, 1899

Found Gold
A farmer Struck It
While Digging A Well

SAN ANTONIO- A farmer residing thirty miles from this city in Bexar County, reports that in digging a well last week at a depth of four feet he struck a vein of peculiar colored rock which extended down for four feet and in which was visible small threads of gold. He has had some of the stuff in the city with him and has been exhibiting it.

—San Antonio Daily Light
January 3, 1900

❖ ❖ ❖

Dead Animals
Have Their Hides
And Flesh Removed.
A Horse And Mule
Recently Treated This Way.
Only Hindquarters
Of The Horse Taken.

SAN ANTONIO- *The Light* recently created a sensation by publishing an account of the trial in Recorder's court of a proprietor of a chili stand who was charged with taking meat from a dead horse.

That was several months ago and the matter had been almost forgotten, but another case similar to the above bobs up again, this time, the hind-quarters of a dead horse, as before have been removed, but there is no proof that a chili manufacture got it. However, it looks suspicious and the facts are as follows:

Wednesday morning while riding towards West End Poundmaster Christian Heuschkel saw a horse almost dead lying in a fit near the Atazan Creek, just east of the old brick factory. Thursday morning he was out that way again and rode over to see what had become of the animal. Its carcass was there, but minus the ski and both hind-quarters, and it looked as if it had only been skinned a short while before he came up. Two or three dogs were present feasting on the forepart of the dead animal and as the skin had been carefully removed they were having a genuine picnic.

Mr. Heuschkel told the above to *The Light* reporter in the city hall in the presence of Captain John Wilkend Jr., whom it remained of a case that recently came into his own knowledge. The captain had a fine mule to die of colic one evening late and he allowed the animal to lie in the stable lot until the next morning when it had swollen to immense proportions. It was then hauled out into the brush and thrown out. The next morning the captain passed the place where it had been dumped and only found the head, bones and entrails of the animal.

—San Antonio Daily Light
January 5, 1900

❖ ❖ ❖

Mastodon Tooth Found

SAN ANTONIO- Mr. S. Rogers with his gang of laborers, while excavating gravel from the Elmendorf gravel pit near the city a few days ago, unearthed a perfect specimen of a mastodon's tooth, which was dug out, roots and all. It must have been once owned by a very large old mammoth, as the tooth is quite large and is much worn, showing however the smooth ivory surface it had in life, probably in the days when Atlantis was a populous continent on earth.

—*San Antonio Daily Light*
February 8, 1900

❖ ❖ ❖

A Boy With A Charmed Life
Lightning Burns One Side Of His Body, But Kills Instantly The Horse He Was Riding.

CANYON- A very remarkable coincidence occurred here yesterday evening. Bud, the 10-year-old son of W.E. Stewart, was out on a horse when a rain, preceded by an electrical storm, came up. Lightning struck the little fellow, burning one side of his hat, tearing one leg of his trousers nearly off, entering his saddle, scorching the lining of the saddle, burning a small hole in the blanket and killing the horse he was riding. The boy was burned about the neck and cheek, and, though much stunned, recovered consciousness and is now fast improving.

—*Dallas Morning News*
July 12, 1900

❖ ❖ ❖

Wrong Name On Tombstone
Man Thought Dead Two Years Turns Up In El Paso And Startles His Friends

EL PASO- John S. Hardwick of Santa Fe N.M. who the mortuary records of El Paso show committed suicide and was buried here in 1898, is a live man and has shocked his friends by appearing on the scene here to-day. Hardwick was a member of Roosevelt's Rough Riders from New Mexico, and after being mustered out came to El Paso. Soon afterward be became mentally deranged and was taken to the hospital here from where he mysteriously escaped. After a long search a body that was positively identified as his was found about five miles from town. A verdict of suicide was rendered and the body buried with military honors and the grave has repeatedly since been decorated with those of other soldiers. Hardwick explains that he found himself in Mexico after leaving here and has entirely recovered. Who the dead man found could have been is a mystery.

—*Dallas Morning News*
September 2, 1900

❖ ❖ ❖

Buried In The Same Coffin
A Woman And Her Child Burned To Death In The Territory

SHERMAN- Further particulars of the burning of Mrs. Jack Williams and little child at South Canadian, OK., are that she was lighting a fire and used a coal oil lamp. The clothing of the infant ignited from that of the mother. Mrs. Williams died at 10 o'clock Monday night and the little one yesterday. They were buried today so a message states, in the same coffin.

—*Dallas Morning News*
September 27, 1900

Kountz Peak
Either A Remarkable Freak Of Nature Or A Marvelous Work Of An Earlier Race

BRENHAM- *The News* correspondent returned last night from "Bear Pond" in Burleson County, where he had been with major. J.T. and Dr. T.C. Houston of Independence and son Harry on a four days' successful duck hunt. A great number of fine mallards were bagged and numbers killed that were never retrieved.

En route to the pond Kountz Peak was visited. This mountain is perhaps 1000 or 1200 feet above sea level, and is the highest point in south or central Texas. The peak was named in honor of Mr. Henry Kountz who settled in Washington County

in 1814. Kountz Creek, in Washington County, and Kountz Bayou, in Burleson County, are named also in honor of this Texas pioneer and patriot, who rendered much valuable civil and military services to the struggling colonists and young republic of Texas. He was one of the numerous modest and unobtrusive heroes, of whose life and distinguished services to the republic and early settlers the historians of Texas fail to give any account.

Kountz Peak is very interesting from every point of view, and from some remarkable. It is a solid, rocky ledge, about one mile long, and notwithstanding its stony nature, forest growth, such as hickory, post oak, pin oak and many smaller varieties of trees attain great size and perfection. It may be said to be a solid mountain of rock, although there is no other rock in that part of Burleson County.

From the summit, when the atmospheric conditions are favorable, large portions of the county, and many of the towns in Grimes, Brazos, Burleson and Washington counties can be seen, and it commands an uninterrupted sweep of the Brazos Valley north and south for fifty miles. The north side is a perpendicular bluff, against which the Brazos bottom joins itself and suddenly terminates, and the general aspect and topographical features of the country change rapidly and completely as if one had been tossed from the depths of the sea to the top of Pike's Peak.

On the north side of the peak the walls are in many places, and for hundreds of feet, perpendicular to the fraction of an inch. This wall is not a solid rock nor is it in stratus or "layers," but is built of blocks of uniform size, and presents precisely the same appearance of the walls of a cut, stone building mortar, seams and all. The similarity is so perfect that if an expert rock mason were shut off from the surrounding, he would declare without hesitation or doubt the masonry was the work of man, and not a natural formation.

Another remarkable feature of this wall, and many of the large flat stones at the top, is that observed closely almost any letter in the alphabet can be seen with the utmost distinctness, and in some places a human face can be easily traced as on the columns in the rotunda of the capital at Washington. This correspondent, after observing it for some time looked for a capital H, and found the letter as perfectly formed as any penman could make it.

The face on this wall presents a dingy, weather beaten appearance, and looks as if it might be 10,000 years old. There have been many theories as to how this great freak of nature was formed. Some say by volcanic eruption, others by a terrible seismic disturbance, and some believe that in the dim ages of the past it was built by some mighty nation of prehistoric people as a breastwork or ordination. No opinion is ventured by this correspondent as to how it was formed, when, by whom, or for what purpose, but the skillful, workman-like manner in which it is constructed makes it one of the remarkable natural, or unnatural objects for which Texas is noted.

The stone in this mountain is apparently of good quality, with one mile of the Conroe branch of the Santa Fe read, and if devel-

oped would furnish much valuable material for jetties and other necessary work for out Texas coast cities.

—*The Galveston Daily News*
December 3, 1900

Log Buried Sixteen Feet
When The Drill Passed Through It A Body Of Water Was Found

CHICOTA- While Jack Walker of Chicota was boring a well for Bob Burroughs north of Paris near Saunders Creek he encountered a log at a depth of sixteen feet. The wood was twenty-four inches thick, and just after getting through it quicksand and an abundant stream of water was struck. The bits of wood pulled up on the drill indicated that the log was petrified or rotten, but in a good state of preservation. Forest trees half a century or a century old were growing all around the spot and the mystery is how the tree could have gotten so far beneath the surface.

—*Dallas Morning News*
February 6, 1901

❖ ❖ ❖

Petrified Body
Was Stolen
Remarkable Case At Beaumont,
As Narrated By
A Son Of The Deceased.

BEAUMONT- The petrified body of a man has been discovered in Magnolia Cemetery, and since the discovery the body has been stolen from the grave and its present whereabouts are a complete mystery to the relatives of the deceased.

The story is not new, although it has never been published, and the details of the remarkable case were obtained from the relatives of the deceased. The information comes from C.J. Davis, oldest son of the dead man, and is given in the following language:

"My father, G.W. Davis, was a car repairer for the Gulf, Beaumont and Kansas City Railway for a number of years. In February 1900, he became ill with Bright's disease, and on Feb. 7, death resulted. The body was interred in Magnolia Cemetery. It was the first time we had occasion to use a lot in the cemetery, and the body was laid to rest in an obscure spot for the time being. Later we purchased a lot and prepared to remove the body to its new resting place. About three months ago J.R. Carroll, an intimate friend of my father and of the family, procured assistance and went to the cemetery to transfer the remains to the private lot. The assistance employed by Mr. Carroll soon opened the grave to the coffin, and they were surprised to find that the bottom of the grave was filled with eighteen or twenty inches of water, which was slightly discolored.

"The water was taken out and they attempted to raise the coffin, but were yet more surprised to find that they were unable to do so, although they combined their efforts. This so mystified them that they took off the plate which covered the glass over the face and shoulders of the body, and found that the body had become petrified as solid as marble. The corpse was not in the least decomposed save that part of the upper lip was gone. The face, shoulders, head, and in fact, every part of the body from the waist line up, being as much as they could see through the glass, was as perfectly formed as though it had been chiseled from stone. Even the eyes were intact, and the hands, which were folded across the breast, were joined solidly together. There was no hair on the head or face. The clothing had fallen away from the body and left it clearly exposed. The substance was perfectly white and firmly made, and not, as in some instances of this sort, of a porous formation.

"After making this examination, Mr. Carroll obtained more assistance and the body was removed and buried in the new grave, without making further examination. There was no effort to keep the matter secret. This was three months or more ago that we discovered the condition of the body. In the meantime my mother had been approached by some parties in the city who offered to buy the body, but she would not entertain the idea, and steadfastly refused to talk with them. They persisted made an offer of $4,000, but my mother still refused to consider the proposition.

"We finally concluded to take up the body and, if it was found to be in a perfect state of petrifaction, to bring it home with us. Accordingly last Sunday, with my mother, Mrs. Carroll, some other gentlemen and some young ladies, we went to the cemetery for the purpose of exhuming the body. When we approached the sexton of the cemetery and acquainted him with our intention he was very much opposed to the idea, and the more we persisted the more he argued against opening the grave. He gave numerous reasons why the body should not be moved and said that bodies have been known to evaporate when brought to the surface of the ground. At any rate, we determined to carry out our original intention, and particularly in view of the fact that there were signs about the grave which seemed to indicate that it had been tampered with. The soil was not as compactly set as it should have been, and Mr. Carroll, who made the grave, was almost certain that it had been molested. We finally opened the grave, to find that the corpse was gone.

"The lid of the coffin had been removed and replaced, and the boards which are placed across the top of the coffin to prevent the weight of the earth from crushing it were gone. The coffin was not taken out, and the bits of cloth and other things which were there were not removed, but not a sign of the body could be found, and until this minute we know nothing about its whereabouts, or have we the slightest clue as to who could have stolen it. Of course we have not made an extensive search, and there is no question that the robbers laid their plans well and too deeply for us to fathom them without the help of expert detectives and a systematic and costly search. And here rests the mystery."

Mr. C.J. Davis, who gave the above story to *The News* representative, is employed at the machine shops of the Beaumont Iron Works. He resides with his mother at 1474 Laurel avenue. The family of Mrs. Davis consists of two sons and six daughters. Two of the daughters are married and the other four live at home.

Mr. J. R. Carroll, who exhumed the body originally and saw it, is employed with Mr. S.A. McNeeley as claim agent. Mr. Davis and others say that Mr. Carroll will testify to the above facts and that the body was perfectly petrified. Others with Mr. Carroll at the time the body was removed were not known to him. He hired them for a few hours and knew neither their names nor anything about them. G.W. Davis, the deceased, was 46 years old at death and was a man about 5 feet 6 or 8 inches and weighed 136 pounds.

—*Dallas Morning News*
July 7, 1901

❖ ❖ ❖

Found An Old Style Coffin
Paris' Sherlock Holmes Have A Mystery To Solve

PARIS- John Argo, one of the clerks at the Paris Hardware Company's store at the corner of Grand Avenue and Short Street, made a mysterious find this morning. Half way back from the front at the side of the building he discovered a narrow pine box with a hasp and padlock fastening. The hasp was broken and on raising the top of the box a queerly shaped coffin was revealed. It looked to be about the size necessary to bury a 12-year-old child in it. It had a flat cover with a glass fencing at the head and had wooden handles. It was covered with dirt and cobwebs. While there is no doubt about its being a coffin, it is decided queer and antiquated. It has been suggested that it is probably part of the paraphernalia of some secret lodge-room. As to how it came to be where it was found is a mystery. A negro is said to have been seen to deposit the box in the street yesterday, but nobody paid any attention to what it contained.

—*Dallas Morning News*
August 14, 1901

EXTRA! EXTRA!

The town of Sebree was in southern Jack County. It is believed to have been settled in the middle to late 1880s. By the 1940s, Sebree no longer existed.

❖ ❖ ❖

Got An Empty Coffin
Queer Present For Ellis County Commissioners Came By Express

WAXAHACHIE- Yesterday a large box such as is used for shipping coffins was received by one of the express companies here addressed to the county officers. No name or address of a consignor was on it, and whom it came from is a mystery. Upon being opened the box was found to contain an empty pauper's coffin. The county officers were notified, but all disclaimed any interest, and denied having ordered such an article. It is supposed to be the work of some practical joker.

—*Dallas Morning New*
January 1, 1902

Petrified Buffalo Skull Found

SEBREE- While out hunting Saturday evening on Jasper Creek, sixteen miles east of Jacksboro, I found the forehead and horns of a monster buffalo, which is petrified and is a solid rock. It was about five feet under the ground. Men who have seen it say it is the largest of the kind they ever saw. It measures thirteen inches from eye to eye and eleven inches across the neck bone behind the horns. It is a solid rock and its forms are natural as life. The pith of the horns are solid. The skull weighs about thirty pounds.

—*Dallas Morning News*
June 30, 1902

HIDDEN HEADLINES of TEXAS

Phenomenon At Beaumont
Well In Close Proximity To A Duster Spouts Oil To A Height Of Forty Feet

BEAUMONT- The Horseshoe Oil Company's well in block 32 of the Keithward tract gave an exhibition yesterday afternoon that has placed it in the category of Spindletop's phenomena. The well is managed by A.B. Wood and was being bailed at the time. It commenced spouting oil while the bailing process was being carried on, and before it was shut in the oil raised to a height of forty feet, going over the top of the derrick.

This well is decidedly a freak, when it is taken into consideration that a well in close proximity to it, in the same tract which has been drilled to a depth of 874 feet, has not yet shown any signs of oil. Not even any water has shown up in the well. The drillers have set the casing and the well should be in. However it will be drilled deeper.

Spindletop has sprung innumerable surprises on those who have operated on the hill since the Lucas gusher startled the world, but this gushing well and a dry one hard by at this stage of the development have added to the mystery that had baffled science in the past. The Yellow Pine tract is now considered about the best territory on the hill and considerable drilling is going on there.

—*Dallas Morning News*
November 30, 1902

Searching For Buried Treasure
Mysterious Excavation Made Of Farm Near McKinney

MCKINNEY- A mysterious excavation was made last Friday night on Johnsons Branch, a quarter of a mile west of the public square in the corner of Crease Graves' farm. It was evidently a search for buried treasure.

Old barrel staves and rusty iron hoops were found nearby which bore the appearance of having been buried many years. The hole appeared to have been eight or ten feet down, as it had filled in with chunks and logs several feet long.
The dirt was too muddy and clammy to be thrown out again at present, but will be examined as soon as it dries some. Many years ago, an old Indian or Mexican trail passed one spot, and it is the memory of old settlers that treasure was buried here by someone who returned to recover it. The spot is marked by an old pecan tree eighteen inches in diameter that had been cut with an ax, and an augur hole bored through the body.

—*The Galveston Daily News*
March 6, 1903

❖ ❖ ❖

Freak At Echo
Artesian Water And Oil Issue From Well Recently Bored

ECHO- A peculiar freak of nature is occurring at the well recently bored by the Southern Pacific Railroad Company at

Echo. The well is producing 80,000 barrels of artesian water daily and for two days now oil has been oozing in considerable quantities from the pipe. The flow of oil seems to be increasing each day instead of diminishing.

Many oil enthusiasts from Orange visited the well and are firmer than ever in their belief that oil in great quantities exists in Orange County. The first well is to be sunk next week by the Orange Oil and Refining Company, who have been busy all the week erecting their derricks and getting the machinery on the grounds.

—*Dallas Morning News*
August 8, 1903

❖ ❖ ❖

Shooting At Navasota
Same Bullet Wounds Two Men, Both Of Them Seriously.

NAVASOTA- Last night while the Christmas festivities were in full blast, there occurred on Railroad Street a shooting, the particulars of which, despite the efforts of *The News* correspondent, it is impossible to obtain at present.

The result is that W.E. Hoyle, proprietor of the Hotel Hoyle, lies confined to his bed in the hotel with a serious though not dangerous bullet wound through the back of his neck, and Bob Howard, a former cook at a restaurant, is in a room over a saloon with a dangerous wound in the groin.

Only one shot was fired. The bullet, after entering Hoyle's neck passed out through his shoulder and struck Howard in the groin. Later in the night Fletcher Leake was arrested, charged with the shooting. He gave bond and was released.

—*The Dallas Morning News*
December 26, 1903

❖ ❖ ❖

Farmer Finds Watch
Fifteen Timepieces Discovered Near Sulphur Springs

SULPHUR SPRINGS- Yesterday Aaron Baxley found on his farm, seven miles east of town, fifteen watches. This farm is located near the Missouri, Kansas and Texas Railway track and on the north side of the railroad. The watches were found in some newly cleared ground, and from appearance have been buried several years. Seven or eight of them were silver watches, with Elgin movements. The others looked as though the cases were brass. One of them when wound up ran all night. The others looked as though the movements were ruined.

When or how these watches came to where they were found is a mystery. There are no claimants here, nor has there been a jewelry store robbed in this county for several years.

—*Dallas Morning News*
January 29, 1904

❖ ❖ ❖

Skeleton Of A Mammoth
Bones Of A Monster Animal
Brought To Light

NEWLIN- Last Thursday, while riding over his pasture, G.W. Helm of Childress County, in company with T.M. Pyle of Hall County, found the skeleton of a prehistoric animal. Its frame was fifteen feet in length and the hip joints were as large as a man's head. The ribs were about five feet in length and six inches in circumference. The skeleton is in a partially petrified state. It was found about ten feet under the surface of the ground on the bank.

—*Dallas Morning News*
May 3, 1904

❖ ❖ ❖

Remarkable Coincidences
R.B. Godley, His Son
And His Grandson
Celebrate Birthday At Once.

DALLAS- A remarkable chain of coincidences is reported in the family of R.B. Godley, a well-known resident of Dallas, and a commemorator of the event was had Thursday, when R.B. Godley, E.V. Godley and E.B. Godley celebrated the anniversaries of their births.

R.B. Godley was born on the 28th of September, 1854. On the same day of the month, twenty-three years later, his first son, E.V. Godley, was born, and the coincidence ran into the third generation, on Sept. 28, 1903, when E.B. Godley, was presented as the first born of E.V. Godley, and the first grandson of R.B. Godley.

It is the first case reported where father, son, and grandson were born on the same day of the month and the opportunity to commemorate the triple coincidences came Thursday, when R.B. Godley was 50 years old, his son 27 and his grandson just 1 year of age. The affair was celebrated with a stag supper at the residence of the eldest Godley and covers were laid for ten.

—*Dallas Morning News*
October 2, 1904

Believe It A Bomb
Chief Of Police Has Bit Of Metal
That Is Shunned

FORT WORTH- Chief of Police William Rea has in his desk an innocent-looking little piece of metal, about an inch long and which has the appearance of a miniature

jug, which he believes to be "loaded." It was picked up in an express car and turned over to the chief by the express messenger, who thought that it might contain dynamite or nitroglycerin. Several persons have inspected it, but none has been sufficiently interested to beak it open. At the small end is what appears to be a cap. By tapping it on the outside it is evident that it is hollow, but just what it contains is a mystery which none of the officers care to solve at this time.

—*Dallas Morning News*
February 1, 1905

❖ ❖ ❖

Coincidence In Accident
Brothers Have Similar Misfortunes At Same Time

FORT WORTH- The unusual situation of two brothers, living in one section of the city, each having a painful accident to his foot in places removed from each other on the afternoon of the same day, came to light here to-day. Lewis and Mark Johns, living in North Fort Worth, were the victims. Lewis, who is a switchman on the Fort Worth Belt Railway, had his foot caught in a frog, and by the merest chances got it out before a car ran it over. His shoe was torn to pieces. Mack, who is employed at Swift & Co.'s packing plant, ran a nail through one of his feet.

—*Dallas Morning News*
May 6, 1905

❖ ❖ ❖

Coincidence In Accidents
Miss Kendall And Miss Adams Sustain Injuries At Fair Grounds

DALLAS- A coincidence in accidents occurred at the Fair Grounds last night. Miss Lottie Kendall, prima donna of the Olympia Opera Company, tripped and fell on the auditorium stage during the production of "Boccaccio," sustaining injuries that required the attention of a physician. The latter had scarcely finished attending Miss Kendall when he was summoned to attend Miss Clara Mae Adams, prima donna of the Bagdad company, who was the victim of a similar accident on the stage of "Beautiful Bagdad."

The physician who attended to the injuries of both ladies was a practitioner from an adjoining city, who was visiting the Fair, and happened to be in the auditorium at the time of the accident to Miss Kendall. He stated that neither lady was seriously injured, but that each had sustained a severe shock. Miss Adams was said to be the most severely hurt. She suffered several contusions of the inner portion of the right knee joint and a wrenching of her right side. Both ladies were carried to their apartments in carriages, but not until each had acted her part in the play to the fall of the curtain.

—*Dallas Morning News*
November 11, 1905

❖ ❖ ❖

HIDDEN HEADLINES of TEXAS

Rat Steals Money For Nest
Rodent Lines His Homes With Currency Of A Face Value Of One Hundred Dollars

DALLAS- The discovery of a rat's nest constructed of currency in bills ranging in denomination from $5 to $20 and lined with a check for $22.50 solved a mystery that had hovered about the establishment of George W. Loomis on Main Street. At several different times, covering a period of two or three months, currency was missing from a cash drawer in the bar and as the bartenders were old and trusted employees it could not be figured out how the money had disappeared. The irregularities kept occurring however, until the affair began to look serious.

Yesterday a $5 bill, which it was known had been put down in the bottom part of the drawer only a few hours before, was found dragged across the till and showing some kind of marks. An investigation began and resulted in the discovery of a rat's nest of all the missing currency stored away at the bottom of the big case. The rat had been exceedingly discriminate in his financiering project and had passed all other kinds of paper for the currency, "feathering the nest" with only gold and silver certificates. Several of the bills had been badly mutilated and one $5 certificate was eaten into the little bits, but luckily the number was remaining and it is still redeemable.

Exclusive of a check for $22.50, which formed the lining of the nest, the home of the rat could have been cashed at any bank for $100.

—*Dallas Morning News*
November 16, 1905

❖ ❖ ❖

Robbed In A Graveyard

HOUSTON- While stooping over a grave which she had been decorating in the German Cemetery this afternoon, Mrs. Blackeney was struck over the head with a club in the hands of a negro who had crept from behind. She was knocked unconscious and her assailant grabbed her purse and took to his heels. Another negro, a helper around the graveyard, gave chase, but was unable to overhaul the robber.

—*Dallas Morning News*
July 1, 1906

❖ ❖ ❖

Burglar Was A Goat
Patrolmen Get Hurry Up Call For Burglars And Find A Goat Holding The Fort

DALLAS- "Please come at once to Gould Street. There is a man walking around upstairs and sometimes it sounds like several men. They have turned over the wardrobe and some other things. I've heard them fall. Come at once, for I'm scared nearly to death." This was a message received last night at the police station.

Mounted Officers Garrison and Fanning

PAGE 108

mounted horses and rushed to the place. They were met at the door by a breathless woman, white and trembling. "He almost kicked the panel of the door out a little while ago," she said, "and he swore awfully." "If it's more than one they are all mad. They talk a good deal because they know I am alone in the house."

They left her weeping and imploring them to be careful. One climbed the stairway to the third floor, while the other climbed the back porch pillars, mounted to the roof of the second story and made for a window. As Mr. Garrison peered through the window he heard Mr. Fanning shove the door open and demanded a surrender. Out of the darkness loomed a form. Mr. Fanning was struck amidships and fouled and rendered unseaworthy. Down the stairway bounded a goat, making a noise like an army in headlong retreat. How the goat got there is a mystery, but a small boy in the house and his playmates next door know who got the blame and consequences.

—*Dallas Morning News*
November 23, 1906

❖ ❖ ❖

Find Leg In Streets

HOUSTON- Considerable excitement was created by the finding of a human leg on one of the streets of the First Ward. It started sundry reports and the police were notified. The leg was inspected, but no one could tell where it came from or could explain the mystery. The police connected up with the undertakers and found and that

a man's leg had been cut off by the wheels of a train.

—*Dallas Morning News*
January 9, 1907

❖ ❖ ❖

Finds Tooth Of Mastodon
Man Excavating Gravel Digs Up Molar Near Kerryville

KERRYVILLE- A mastodon's tooth, 76 inches long, 22 inches in circumference and weighing 160 pounds, has been excavated here. It was discovered by W.N. Newton while excavating gravel. It is in a fine state of preservation and is now on exhibition here. Considerable gravel is to be excavated over the same area, and those in charge will attempt to locate other bones of the monster animal. In the same pit other fragments of bones have been uncovered, and some think that this gravel pit may be like some discoveries in other western states, the burying ground of some of the great prehistoric monsters.

—*Dallas Morning News*
January 16, 1907

Probably Tooth Of Monster
Observer Landis Of Weather Bureau Makes Estimate Regarding Find

FORT WORTH- D.S. Landis, official in charge of the local weather bureau, has estimated by careful mathematical computation, that the gigantic tooth brought to

the city recently by Kit Cowan of Wichita Falls, which was dug up in the banks of the Pease River, belonged to an animal thirty feet long, 15 feet high and weighing thirty-eight tons. Photographs of the huge tooth will be sent to the Smithsonian Institution.

—*Dallas Morning News*
December 28, 1907

❖ ❖ ❖

Violating Sunday Law

GALVESTON- Two arrests for violating the Sunday law were recorded on the police blotter yesterday, F. Defarari and Ike O'Donell, the former doing business at Tremont and Strand and the latter at 2501 Strand. Both claim to have been in their places of business making preparations for Monday and that they were not violating the law.

—*The Galveston Daily News*
April 5, 1909

❖ ❖ ❖

Freak Of Nature At Comanche

COMANCHE- Comanche can probably claim the distinction of the queerest shaped tree in Texas. The tree is a double pecan growing on the north bank of Indian Creek about half a mile from the business part of town. The main trunk of the tree comes out of the ground as shown at the right hand side of the picture and bending over in a half circles goes back into the ground, where it is firmly rooted again.

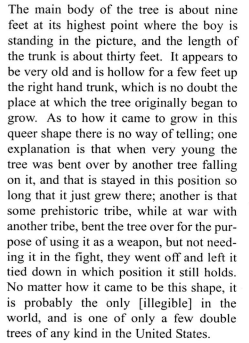

The main body of the tree is about nine feet at its highest point where the boy is standing in the picture, and the length of the trunk is about thirty feet. It appears to be very old and is hollow for a few feet up the right hand trunk, which is no doubt the place at which the tree originally began to grow. As to how it came to grow in this queer shape there is no way of telling; one explanation is that when very young the tree was bent over by another tree falling on it, and that is stayed in this position so long that it just grew there; another is that some prehistoric tribe, while at war with another tribe, bent the tree over for the purpose of using it as a weapon, but not needing it in the fight, they went off and left it tied down in which position it still holds. No matter how it came to be this shape, it is probably the only [illegible] in the world, and is one of only a few double trees of any kind in the United States.

—*Dallas Morning News*
May 15, 1910

Strange Man

MILFORD- A man named Plunkett, aware of the absence of his neighbor from his home, crawled into the man's wife's bed, passing himself as the husband of the woman. In putting her arm around his neck she felt the "biled shirt" of the intruder, and passing her hand over the bosom of shirt felt shirt studs; and knowing her husband wore none, she sprang from bed and called for help. Plunkett ran, but was subsequently captured and committed to jail.

—*The Galveston Daily News*
December 6, 1878

❖ ❖ ❖

A Human Deformity

WAXAHACHIE- The most terrible exhibition of human deformity was seen on our streets this week in the person of a man from Johnson County, who possesses so many of the peculiarities of a serpent, that the most careless glance at him is sufficient to suggest the strange resemblance. His eyes snap and sparkle and look long like those of a snake, his tongue protrudes in frequent quick motions from his mouth, while every muscle and joint of his frame is constantly twisting and writing. There seems to be no strength in any joint. The motions of the body differ from the nervous jerking often seen in persons, in being rather a continual twisting and wiggling rather than anything like the quick contraction and relaxation of muscles.

What is still more wonderful about this monstrosity is that he is possessed of good sense, and is perfectly capable of attending to business—in fact, he is said to own a very nice farm and to superintend its cultivation. He visited our town on business, purchasing corn of Bullard & Adkerson, groceries of Messer. Starf, and dry goods of Mr. H.W. Tippet, which all of whom he traded in a sensible manner, getting the money from his own pocket, and never failing to insist upon a reduction of prices; and your correspondent refers to the above gentlemen for the accuracy of his description. The unfortunate man crawls upon his hands and feet, but in doing so describes a [rest of article illegible].

—*The Galveston Daily News*
June 2, 1880

❖ ❖ ❖

A Strange Freak
A Man Surrenders To The Sheriff Claiming To Be A Murderer For Whom A Reward Is Offered

CORSICANA- A man by the name of Moore went to the courthouse to-day and stepped up to Sheriff West and surrendered himself, stating there was a reward of $1500 offered for his arrest; and that he killed a man in Logan, Ohio, and he was tired of being a fugitive from justice. The Sheriff took him into custody and conveyed him to the county jail, where he was locked up for safe keeping. The sheriff then telegraphed the sheriff at Logan Ohio,

for full particulars concerning Moore and received the following reply: "There is no reward offered for Moore's arrest here. Know Moore to be a jeweler by trade and [illegible]."

—*Dallas Morning News*
March 10, 1888

❖ ❖ ❖

Cursed His Mother's Corpse
Astonishing Conduct Of A Man At His Mother's Wake. Watchers Driven From The Coffinside.

HOUSTON- On Sunday morning Mrs. Susan Arto, an old resident, died at her home in the Second Ward. On Monday John Arto, a son of the deceased, was arrested, charged with assault to murder. The affidavit was made against Arto by Mike Shay, his brother-in-law, and by his uncle, William George. Arto this afternoon had a hearing before Judge Railey. The evidence adduced showed that while several ladies and gentlemen were watching the remains of Mrs. Arto on Sunday night, her son John entered the room with an open knife in his hand, and by loud and indecent language frightened all present and compelled them to leave the house with the exception of Messrs. Shay and George. He, it is also alleged, approached the coffin and cursed his dead mother's remains. Shay remonstrated with him, whereupon Arto attempted to stab Shay and succeeded in cutting one of his hands and inflicted a slight wound in his left side. Shay finally knocked him down and bruised him up considerably, and with the assistance of Mr. George brought him to town and lodged him in jail. During the progress of the trial this afternoon, and while Hon. Henry F. Fisher, one of the counsel, was pleading his cause, Arto interrupted the proceedings of the court by stating in an excited and frenzied way that the whole affair was a conspiracy against him and that the witnesses were infamous liars.

Judge Railey imposed a fine upon him of $50 for contempt of court. Upon the conclusion of the examination the accused was bound over in the sum of $750 to the Criminal Court. The prisoner was then taken before Judge Breeding and fined $25 and costs for using lad and abusive language. Arto, after the trial was over, wanted to prefer charges against Shay for assault and battery, but the demand was not entertained by County Attorney Gillespie. Arto has figured conspicuously in the criminal proceedings of this county and Galveston during the past few years, was released from custody about one year ago on a charge of murdering his father-in-law in Galveston, the case being nolle pressed on account of the absence of and death of witnesses.

—*Dallas Morning News*
May 30, 1888

❖ ❖ ❖

Outgrew His Coffin
Death Of C.J. Veuroux, An Eccentric Citizen Of La Belle France.

SAN ANTONIO- Last night C.J. Veuroux died in the 74th year of his age. There was nothing in particular the matter with him beyond his advanced span. He was a Frenchman by birth, a locksmith by trade, and universally respected. Eighteen years ago he made himself a coffin of iron. It stood in his working place in view of all visitors. He was very proud of its workmanship, its shape, the elegant manner in which it fit him and its other merits.

He realized a handsome competency and retired from the business taking his future coffin with him. Up to the moment of his death it was a cherished piece of furniture in his bedchamber. He never lost faith in it and his admiration of it never abated a jot. Unfortunately, like most of his nation, he took on much flesh. When the attendants attempted to place him in the "narrow house" which his hands had fashioned so many years ago it was found that he had overgrown it. All efforts were unavailing and C.J. Veuroux was buried in a custom-made coffin after all.

—*Dallas Morning News*
July 7, 1888

❖ ❖ ❖

Freaks In Marriage

GALVESTON- The marriage on Tuesday in a dime museum, of a female "freak" weighing 650 pounds avoirdupois, to a male "freak" weighing 90 pounds avoirdupois, is not precisely the sort of a marriage, all the circumstances considered, which the believers in the capacity of home life can contemplate with the greatest satisfaction. But many a so-called "marriage in high life" is no less grotesque.

—*The Galveston Daily News*
March 1, 1889

EXTRA! EXTRA!

The worst natural disaster in United States history was caused by a hurricane that hit Galveston in 1900. Over 8000 deaths were recorded.

Scalps Brought In
By A Youth Of Six Summers, Who Killed The Beasts Himself. Small Pay.

SAN ANTONIO- Martin Hernandez, a Mexican boy aged six years, who resides on the Leon Creek at the Dwyer ranch, came in this morning and delivered to County Judge McAllister, the scalps of a large coyote and a good sized wild cat, both of which animals the boy had killed with his own hands, but under the law, he only got $1, and had to ride fourteen miles for it after having killed the wild beasts.

—*Fort Worth Gazette*
April 23, 1891

❖ ❖ ❖

Carries His Coffin
Along With Him, Wants To Be Buried In It.

HARROLD- T.H. Weatherford, a man 81 years old, who has been living south of here for some time, created considerable curiosity here to-day by having a box made of pine, 6 feet long, two feet wide and 2 feet high, checked to Dallas, Tex. He had it made for his coffin, some five years ago, at Macon City, Mo., and takes it with him wherever he goes and says he wants to be buried in it, just as it is.

—*Dallas Morning News*
October 8, 1891

❖ ❖ ❖

Didn't Know How He Got There
Where Pat's Jag Left Him

BRENHAM- A native of Hibernis was discovered in a queer situation at 3 o'clock this morning. He was found on top of one of the awnings on Main Street. An early riser heard him walking around on the tin roof and called to him, asking what he was doing up there. He replied that he didn't know but he thought somebody must have

PAGE 115

put him there, and he didn't know how to get down; it was either that or else the house was haunted and the ghosts had carried him there. He had been drunk, he said, the night before, and when he came to himself he was on top of the awning. Marshal Swain assisted him down and he went his way rejoicing.

—*Dallas Morning News*
February 26, 1892

❖ ❖ ❖

Hermit Of The Woods
Supposed Escaped Convict Chasing Boys Near Waco

WACO- Along a range of hills southeast of Lorena is a strip of chaparral a mile wide and several miles in length. It is impenetrable except by narrow and sinuous paths, so thick is the growth of scrubby oaks, interlaced with vines. Boys threading these paths report being chased by a ragged man with long hair and beard, armed with a club. As these reports are believed, the citizens have been searching the chaparral several days in an organized posse. The theory is that this terror of the brush is a state convict who escaped a year ago from a gang employed in the Missouri, Kansas and Texas railway. The escape occurred a few miles from the haunted chaparral. A hut has been found in a dense portion of the oaks and strewed about it were bones of animals. The search will be continued until the mystery is explained.

—*Dallas Morning News*
April 8, 1893

❖ ❖ ❖

A Texas Hermit

WILLOW CREEK- Wilbarger County has long been rife with stories of a mysterious recluse who is known as the "Veiled Hermit." His dwelling place is near Willow Creek, in the county named, in a cave partly natural and partly excavated by him. This cave is lined with skin and decorated with drawings on the wall, the work of the hermit himself, and showing marked taste and talent as an artist.

The hermit, who has lived in the cave for the past seventeen years, always wears a close fitting mask of buckskin, which, falling to the waist, completely hides his face. He dresses in skins in the winter, while in the summer he is clad in a loose garment woven of prairie grass. He subsists upon the game which he gathers by hunting and fishing and the produce of a small tract of ground which he cultivates near his cave. He is never seen save at long intervals, and when accosted by accident replies in monosyllables to all questions and retires as soon as possible. Nothing is known of his antecedents, but those who have met him say that his conversation and bearing show him to be an Englishman of the better class.

—*Dallas Morning News*
June 16, 1893

❖ ❖ ❖

One Hundred And Fifteen Years Old

SAN ANTONIO- W. H. Jones presented the Messenger with a tin-type picture of the historic old Madame Candelaria, who was one of the three females in the Alamo when the Texas patriots were massacred by Santa Anna's army on March 6, 1836, she having been employed, she said by Gen. Sam Houston, to nurse Bowie, who had consumption. This old lady died last month in San Antonio. She was 115 years old last November, she having been born in Nov. 1783. In her death, we lost the last eyewitness of that bloody massacre 63 years ago. Mr. Jones talked with the old lady when in San Antonio 2 years ago and bought a photo from which he had a number of tin-types made. She had been blind several years, but when her photo was taken she had her pet dog in her lap.

—*Rockdale Messenger*
March 2, 1899

❖ ❖ ❖

Wild Man Of Elm Hollow
What Drove The Hermit To The Caves And Caverns Of The Brazos Bottoms

CLEBURNE- A few months ago a description of Elm Hollow, that wild and mountainous region of this county bordering in the Brazos River appeared in these columns, accompanied with an interview with Mr. Clem Pierce as to a hermit who once lived in a cave near there. It was thought then that the old hermit died or disappeared, but the following experience of a crowd of citizens from this city shows that the old [newspaper ends report].

—*Dallas Morning News*
September 13, 1899

Can't Tell Where Home Is

CADDOPEAK- Late Wednesday evening an idiotic boy about 10 years old came to Mr. Coneley's house, near this place. He was barefooted and bareheaded. The child came from a westward street. He can not or will not talk. Whose boy he is or where he came from whether lost or abandoned, is still shrouded in mystery.

—*Dallas Morning News*
July 28, 1900

❖ ❖ ❖

Married The Wrong Brother
Facts Of A Rather Strange Romance Transpire In The Territory

PARIS- A romantic secret marriage, which occurred at Antlers, I.T., came to light a few days ago. A young lady, formerly a resident of Paris, was married about a year ago to a young citizen of the Choctaw Nation, living at Antlers. They were married at Denison. Shortly after the marriage the young couple separated. Neither gave the slightest intimation as to the cause of their separation, which seemed to have been through a mutual understanding, but was regarded as a mystery by their friends and acquaintances.

After their separation the husband brought suit for divorce in the Indian Court last August. The court refused to grant him a divorce. His wife later brought suit and was granted a divorce last month. A few days afterward she was secretly married to a younger brother of the divorced husband. They kept the wedding a secret, however, only a few days.

—*Dallas Morning News*
March 3, 1901

❖ ❖ ❖

Probably Convicted Herself
Indiscreet Course Of A Woman Who Was On Trial As To Her Sanity

CLEBURNE- A good deal of amusement was created in the county court by the remarks of a woman being tried for lunacy. On seeing only six men in the jury box she stated very plainly that it took twelve men to try a case in Georgia. After this she paid her respects to the court, the clerk and the jurymen. The jury found her insane. She was brought here from the eastern part of the country.

—*Dallas Morning News*
December 1, 1901

❖ ❖ ❖

One-Eyed Wild Man

TERRELL- It is reported that a wild man has been seen in the Trinity River bottom near red Bank. He is described as being a tall negro, one-eyed, male and burly all over. When seen the wild man ran and so did the party who saw him. The point where the stranger was seen is in the southern part of this county. [Remainder illegible.]

—*Galveston Daily News*
September 14, 1903

A Wild And Burly Man

RED BANK- A wild and burly man has been seen near Red Bank in Trinity [illegible], in Kaufman County. Why not capture him and have him at the Texas State Fair?

—*Galveston Daily News*
September 16, 1903

❖ ❖ ❖

Biggest Man A Texas Product

BEAUMONT- The other morning at the Frisco tracks in Fort Scott was the biggest man in the world. He is known as "Baby Jim" Simmons, a negro, who weighs 750 pounds. There are but few who believe that any human being could attain such a great weight unless they chanced to see this mastodon.

One glimpse at the monster, however, allays all doubt as to the man's enormous physical proportions. Everyone who saw his massiveness went away telling himself that the negro weighed nearer a ton than the weight before him. "Jim" Simmons was accompanying W. R. MacBurnett, a theatrical circus man, to St. Joseph. The monster lives at Beaumont Tex. He occupied the two seats in the smoker, and slept all the time from early morning until 9 o'clock, though there was a constant stream of people scrambling through the car to see him. Efforts to wake the negro were unsuccessful. He remained there snoring loudly and also breathing heavily. Finally his manager came through the car, cleared out the curious ones and took his big one to the vestibule to give him an airing. A newspaper man was admitted to converse with the mastodon for a few minutes.

Simmons said he was 20 yeas of age, that his parents were both small, though his grandparents each weighed over the 300 mark. He say he does not eat or drink any more than the average-sized man, and that he enjoys the best of health, his heart behaving in a most satisfactory manner. He is but sixty-nine inches tall and is "further around than up and down," to use a small boy's expression. There is no doubt that this man is one of the most gigantic human beings that ever lived.

—*Dallas Morning News*
December 1, 1907

❖ ❖ ❖

Strange Woman Captured
Reported To Have Lived In Hills In Gregg County In Wild State. Taken To Longview.

LONGVIEW- For over a month the people around Elderville, eight miles south of here in this county, have been aroused over the appearance of a wild woman and a few weeks ago a Houston newspaper had a big write up from the Elderville telling of the exploits of this creature, but many thought the whole thing a myth on account of the mysterious and far distant appearance of the wild woman seemingly at the same hour. She was very sly and would only show herself to children and to a single person, always at a safe distance, but in a threatening manner to scare. She seemed to have a grim delight in flitting out of sight and passing rapidly to a distant place and showing herself in order to mystify everyone.

It finally got to a point where negroes would not work in a field unattended and school children were afraid to go to school. The country schools are all taught this time of the year to accommodate farmers, so something must be done and about forty men gathered to search for the creature. They had just organized partly when a messenger arrived and the chase was taken up in earnest, few believing anything real would be captured. She had been described in every imaginable form and shape from a veritable giant to a lion, an as running faster than any express train.

The big posse urged their horses to the place last indicated and sure enough enormous tracks were found in the field leading to a big woods land. Riders were sent around the woodland and men on foot took up the fresh trail and soon found her crouched in a little thicket, where she had been scared from the noise of the horses going around to head her off. When she saw she was discovered in the undergrowth she ran rapidly away, but was caught after a long sprint by W. R. Adams, who was soon assisted by others, and brought to town and put in detention where she will be tried to-morrow for lunacy.

She talked intelligently at times, but would not answer any questions at others. She said her name is Cynthia Goodley, 35 years old; that she is from East Hamilton,

HIDDEN HEADLINES of TEXAS

Sabine County, Tex. She is tall, sinewy, strong and active. She had on a loose-fitting Mother Hubbard only. Her feet were the largest ever seen here and bore evidence of never being shed. Her skin seemed thick and tough, not a bruise or a scratch from long exposure to woods life. She is as black as ebony, of the old African type. She had a small, long sack that would hold about a peck. In it she had a queer mixture of mullen leaves, ink balls, pieces of root, but no food. She has never been known to steal any provisions. How she subsisted is a mystery.

—*Dallas Morning News*
July 15, 1908

He Had A Dream

ALEXANDER- A farmer living near this place dreamed a few nights since that he was to die on Feb. 25, and so firmly is he impressed with the dream that he has made his will and arranged all of his business to meet the grim monster prepared. He says his mother was warned in the same way, and died on the appointed day. His name is S. Wilkins, aged about 50.

—*Dallas Morning News*
February 20, 1886

❖ ❖ ❖

Was It A Miracle?
A Bed-ridden Rheumatic Gets Up And Walks, Saying God Had Cured Him.

MERIDIAN- Henry Scantlin was yesterday adjudged a lunatic. Scantlin is about 38 years of age and unmarried, has lived in the county for eighteen or twenty years, and for the past ten or twelve years been a great sufferer from rheumatism, much of the time being bed ridden, and his muscles were contracted and limbs deformed. Ten days ago he rose from his bed, telling his mother and brother that the Lord had suddenly made him whole. His voice was strong, he stood erect, his step seeming elastic.

The mother and brother were of course astonished and rejoiced. The neighbors, hearing of the miracle, came to see them and there was much excitement in the neighborhood. Several ministers called to see him. It was noticed after a few days that he had symptoms of insanity, which rapidly increased and his brother Newton also showed symptoms that he too lost his mind. Complaints of lunacy were made against both of them. Henry was adjudged insane and Newton discharged, and the mystery surrounding the miracle unexplained to that neighborhood.

—*Dallas Morning News*
November 24, 1889

❖ ❖ ❖

A Spirit Painting
A Landscape In Pale Colors
Painted On A Plaque
By Hands Spiritual.
Attitude Of The Bible Toward
Christians And Spiritualists
Considered Without Partisan Bias
For Or Against.

WACO- Owing to the aversion of the foremost Waco mediums to notoriety, they have declined, although requested by *The News* reporter, to allow the use of their names in mention of the wonderful results witnessed at their séances. In social circles, as well as religious, unexplainable phenomena are constantly under discussion.

Many séances have taken place at residence of Dr. G.C. McGregor, a wealthy retired physician, whose elegant home is located at the corner of Columbus and North Eighth Streets. Dr. McGregor's parlor is the favorite resort of believers and students of spiritualism. On a center table is a plaque painted with a landscape in pale colors, and this painting Dr. McGregor received as a gift from a friend for whom it was painted by the spirit of a friend of his friend under circumstances that exclude from the mind of the doctor and other scientists any theory other than that the pic-

ture is actually as represented, the painting of a phantom artist. Messages are received through slate-writing and from the lips of trance mediums, conveying intelligence between this and the other world in a manner that sets doubt aside.

It was rumored that Mr. J.D. Shaw, the editor of the Independence Pulpit, was a convert to spiritualism, and *The News* reporter called to talk with him. Mr. Shaw remarked that he had not been converted to anything, but had lately been engaged in a controversy with those who held that Christianity and Spiritualism were repellent and incompatible. "Can the Bible be successfully used in defense of modern spiritualism?" *The News* reporter inquired. "I do not regard the Bible as an infallible book," Mr. Shaw replied, "but I think it can be as successfully used in defense of modern Christianity. The Bible is an accommodating book. The Catholics use it in defense of their doctrines, and so do the Episcopalian, the Presbyterians, the Baptists and the Methodists, each one of which differs from all the rest, and with equal latitude for interpretation, I think it may be as successfully used by the spiritualists.

"The spiritualists hold some things in common with the Christians. As to the alleged duel nature of man and spiritual immortality the two systems agree, that is, they both teach that man has a spirit, and that the spirit will survive the organic body, doctrines in defense of which the Bible is worth as much to one as it is to the other. The Spiritualists teach the possibility of spirit return to earth, that we may, and that some do, communicate with them through

human mediums, and this they regard as more convincing evidence of spirit being and immortality than anything to be found in the Bible. Christians, as a rule, deny all this, and base their faith in the future life solely upon the Bible which they regard as an infallible book of divine origin.

"Now I am neither a spiritualist nor a Christian. As to whether or not man had a dual nature, I am in a state of doubt, I do not believe, nor do I know that he has not. Unable to solve the problem of whether or not the spirits as distinct from the body and brain, is a substantial entity, I am, therefore, in doubt about there being a future life. This places me in a situation to consider the attitude of the Bible towards Christians and Spiritualists without any partisan bias in favor or against either. In so far as Christians and Spiritualists agree, the Bible may be quoted as sustaining both of them, but the question to be considered now is, whether or not it sustains the Spiritualists in their claim that we may communicate with the spirits of those who have once lived in the flesh.

"There is no doubt in my mind but that spiritualism is much older than Christianity, and that what we call modern Spiritualism is only a revival of what has existed in one form or another since prehistoric times. The Bible is full of Spiritualism, and seems to have been written by spiritual mediums. Moses and Daniel were writing mediums; the prophets were all clairvoyant and trance mediums, and so was John, the revelator. Samuel and Paul were clairaudient, while Paul was also a healer, and so was Peter. Jesus was a medium for both healing and materialization, he was also a great mind reader and a medium for the development of other mediums; in fact, we find in the Bible instances of nearly every phase of mediumship claimed by the Spiritualists of to-day but before we note these it may be well enough to designate some points of difference between ancient and modern Spiritualism, though these matters are neither so great nor so numerous as those between ancient and modern Christianity.

"Ancient Spiritualists generally attributed the power producing spirit phenomena to God and angels, while modern Spiritualists attribute it mainly to the spirits of persons who have lived upon the earth, though many modern mediums claim that they are influenced by divine power. This difference may be accounted for on the ground of human ignorance as to the true source of this power. What Moses considered to be the finger of God writing up stone tablets was doubtless the same as what a Siade or a Howe now tell us is the finger of some disembodied spirit, writing between closed slates. Anciently many things were attributed to gods and angels that are known to be natural effects of natural causes. While many of the phenomena recorded in the Bible are about the same as those reported to be appearing now, there are a few much more startling and marvelous, for instance, as raising the dead and bringing fire down from heaven, but just how much exaggeration there is in these biblical accounts we cannot determine. One thing we do know is, that among modern spiritualists there is a great tendency to exaggeration.

"The Bible does not use the terms 'circle,' 'séance,' 'clairvoyance,' etc., but it clearly describes what we now call by these names. At a séance given by Jesus, as recorded in the seventeenth chapter of Matthew, the circle consisted of Jesus, Peter, James and John. On that occasion there was what is now called a 'material-ization.' Moses and Elias who had long been dead appeared talking with the medium, spirit light was seen also and a voice was heard. After the death of Jesus he is reported to have appeared in a materialized form on several occasions, two of which as stated in the twenty-fourth chapter of Luke occurred at and near Jerusalem, first to two of his disciples and afterward to the eleven, gathered in a room just as people gather now to 'hold a circle' or 'have a séance.' We have a most striking descrip-tion of a circles and a séance in the first and second chapters of the Acts of the Apostles in which spirit lights were seen, and some of the mediums spoke in other tongues than their own. So it appears that they must have held séances occasionally just as the Spiritualists do now, and, as fur-ther proof that the Spiritualism of the Bible is in many respects similar to what we hear of as existing to-day. I will note a few cases covering the different phases of mediumship, though to note them all would extend this answer beyond a reason-able limit.

"In addition to the materializations already mentioned we have a striking instance in Joshua v. 13-15, where a spirit calling him-self 'captain of the host of the Lord' appeared with a drawn sword. In John xxi. 1-18, we have a full-form materialization of Jesus which occurred some time after his death. For instances of clairvoyance, we refer to the prophecy of Ezekiel and Revelation. In the twenty-second chapter of revelation what John took to be an angel turned out to be the spirit of one of the prophets. These ancient clairvoyants sometimes saw other objects, as in the case of Elisha's young man, whose eyes were opened to see horses and chariots of fire round about his master. Kings vi. 17, Zechariah saw a flying rod twenty cubits long and ten cubits wide and on another occasion he saw four chariots come out from between two mountains. Samuel rep-resented in the I Samuel iii. 4-8 was clairaudient and so was John as reported in the fourth chapter of Revelation.

—*Dallas Morning News*
August 26, 1894

A Communication From Heavens

Received By Mr. C.W. Lawson
On The 4th Of Last July

ENNIS- Mr. C.W. Lawson of Ennis was at the city hall yesterday ready to deliver an interesting lecture on "Man—Where Did He Come from and Where Is He Going To?" but he failed to find an audience and the lecture was indefinitely postponed. Mr. Lawson claims to have received on the 4th of last July the following communication from heaven, which he consents to have published:

A proclamation to the United States of America, greeting: From the living God of heaven through the Elijah spirit he was sent upon earth crying: Prepare ye the way of the Lord. Make his path straight, for he is coming soon to take possession of every kingdom and nation upon this earth. The sooner you heed this the better, for every individual kingdom and nation that will not yield to the iron rule of his word shall be cut off in death and there will be no exemption from this.

First your consent is required as individuals in preparing his way, to believe on him and Jesus Christ, his son, whom he has sent in flesh and blood under two covenant seals of the living God via circumcision on all males from eight days old up and water baptism in the name of the Father, Son, and Holy Ghost. See example Matt, iii. 13-17 with the promise he received from his father's holy spirit upon all his followers in the end to make the marriage covenant complete before the seal of the holy spirit is attached. Second, your consent is required collectively or national, by laying aside national laws and adopting Old Testament laws, which rule individual kingdoms and nations of this world. There will be no exemption from this first and last.

Attest:
His word, "First shall be last."
His spirit, "Last shall be first."
His power to enact the same in the nation and all nations upon earth the same.
Amen.

—*Dallas Morning News*
September 24, 1894

EXTRA! EXTRA!

The town of Ranger was named in honor of the Texas Rangers who had a camp a few miles outside of the town in the 1870s.

Truly Phenomenal

**The Power Of Clairvoyance Or
Mind Reading Possessed By Two
Ranger Children.
Living Protests Against The Views
Of Professor Hyslop.
Doings That Throw Bishop
Into The Shade.**

RANGER- Ranger contains a couple of diminutive prodigies. They are brother and sister, aged respectively 12 and 14 years. Their name is Schram, and their father is a farmer. They have enjoyed meager scholastic advantages, and for the most part have occupied themselves about the cotton fields of their father. But although unskilled in book lore and deficient in conventional training, they are singularly proficient in a species of telepathy, clairvoyance or something, the manifestation of which has given rise to much curious speculation.

The children were here to view the fair, and were the guests of Dr. Gilbert, at Oak Cliff. The doctor soon became aware of their peculiar qualities and head them perform feats of the telepathic order which he describes as little short of the miraculous. Let the doctor tell his experience in his own words:

"The children," he said, "were brought here by my son from Eastland to see the fair. In personal appearance they are not at all extraordinary. Aside from their one singular tendency they possess nothing that would be called precocious. But in mind reading they can give pointers to many who have made a business out of it. I will cite some remarkable instances, and you can think what you please. Having been informed of what they had done in this way, I immediately subjected them to a practical test. I hid a silver dollar in a remote part of the house, and then told them I had lost something which I would like to recover. The little boy then, I thought, acted very curiously. He seemed dazed, stood up and pressed his hands over his eyeballs. He repeated this action several times, then started, lifted his head, and without a faltering a moment, marched directly toward the concealed article, which he brought to me in great triumph. This was the first manifestation."

"Subsequently I wrapped my watch up in some newspapers and very carefully concealed it. The children were absent at the time and could not possibly have been apprised of the hiding place. When they entered the house I casually observed to the boy that I had lost something. Both the boy and girl put their fingers on their eyes, and presently the little girl looked up, smiling brightly and said, 'I don't know what you have hidden, but whatever it is, you have wrapped it up in some newspapers.' Both children then rushed to the hiding place without hesitation and brought me my watch. On another occasion I wished to know what time it was, and before I consulted my watch the boy volunteered to tell me. Up went his hands to his eyes with the same motion, and he told me the time to a second. The children are much given to the performance of such prodigies as their home in Ranger. There they have been known to herald the approach of a visitor, and to give a detailed narrative of his experiences on the road. For instance, my son met them one day at their house and one of the children remarked that he had left something behind. It was a correct surmise. My son had unhitched his horse from the buggy and left it under a great oak tree. The unhitching of the horse, its position under the tree the character of the surroundings country, and other attendant circumstances were accurately detailed by these two singular children."

"The strangest part about it all is the fact that they do not resort to physical contact in order to expedite their search for hidden articles. They wholly dispense with this feature, which was practiced by Bishop and other professional celebrities, and which creates a suspicion of more or less charlatanism. What these children accomplish is destitute of the remotest semblance of legerdemain. There is no apparent effort, no spasmodic straining, no contorting of the face or twisting of the body. There are no gyrations of any sort. They are not conscious of the mysterious power they possess, or if so regard it as inconsequential. It would require a good deal of study and speculation to account for these psychic manifestations. The children are not diseased in any way, have no abnormal development and have light and cheerful dispositions. Whether it is a species of clairvoyance, telepathy or mind reading I cannot say. I do not know how to classify it. I notice that Prof. Hyslop, in an article published in *The News* a few Sundays past contends that all mind reading, as generally understood, is little better than ingenious legerdemain."

"The two children under discussion are living protests against this contention. It is my intention to have these children down here again soon, when I may take occasion to more elaborately investigate their strange powers."

—*Dallas Morning News*
November 8, 1894

❖ ❖ ❖

A Dream Awoke Him
He Finds Men Burglarizing His Store And Routs Them Out

HAWKINS- Burglars entered the store of Bussey, Ayres & Caston about 12 o'clock last night, by prying open the large double doors in front. The circumstances connected with it are, in some respects, a little peculiar. Capt. C.H. Bussey, the senior member of the firm, was awakened from a dream in which it appeared to him that an old brick frame building in the rear of their brick store in which formerly did business, was on fire. In his dream someone had asked him if he was losing anything by the fire, and he answered "Yes, a thousand dollars of oats." There were no oats in the building, nor was it afire, but the captain thinks he must have answered the dream question aloud, and that the sound of his own voice aroused him. So impressed was he with the dream that he went to the front door of his residence and looked out in the direction of the store. He discovered that there was a dim light in the brick store. He dressed himself and reached the front of the store just in time to see one of the burglars disappear around the corner. They were evidently frightened by the approach of the captain, as they left without their booty.

Some neighbors were summoned, and an investigation disclosed the fact that the burglars were preparing to load themselves well. A couple of large valises had been taken from shelves, and one of them was well packed with shoes. Other shoes were found upon the counters, and scattered over the floor, white shirts and other articles which had been taken from the show cases. There is no clew. Capt. Bussey says he don't know how this dream business will look in print, but it's true, every word of it.

—*Dallas Morning News*
July 9, 1896

Hypnotized By Telephone

NAVASOTA- Will Camp, who submitted to the power of a hypnotist there for the cure of cigarette smoking, had occasion to call up the professor by telephone at Bryan yesterday, when the hypnotist put his subject under hypnotic influence over the wire. Skeptics tested the subject with pins

and were convinced of the genuineness of the subject's insensibility to pain.

—*Dallas Morning News*
April 13, 1897

❖ ❖ ❖

Hypnotized By Telegraph
Subject Was Put To Sleep By Suggestion Sent Over The Wires. Was Subjected To Several Tests. Mr. John C. Witt, A Local Telegraph Operator, Was The Hypnotist.

GALVESTON- Hypnotized by telegraph. That feat was performed yesterday afternoon in the editorial rooms of *The News*. Mr. John C. Witt was the hypnotist. Mr. Witt is a telegraph operator employed in the Western Union offices on Strand. In February last, after attending a local hypnotic performance, he became interested in the subject and studied it under a professional hypnotist, with satisfactory results. A short while ago he conceived the idea of hypnotizing a subject by suggestion over the telegraph wires, and arrangements were made to test its possibility yesterday afternoon.

At the hour of 3 o'clock there were assembled in the editorial rooms two subjects, one John Sterling and the other Charles Boehm. There were also present as spectators Charles A. Witt, H. Eldrige, D.J. Clark, a reporter and several of *The News* attaches. Mr. Sam Nolley presided over the telegraph key in *The News* office and received the suggestions over the wire from Mr. Witt, who operated the key in the Western Union office on the Strand, a block away.

Before the experience was commenced Sterling, one of the subjects, stated to the reporter that he was 29 years of age and was born in England. He had been in this country however, for a number of years. By occupation he was a waiter and bartender. He further stated that he was first hypnotized about eight years ago in New York by Prof. Lee, but had been so roughly treated by that gentleman during the exhibitions that he had fought shy of all hypnotic performances ever since. A few days ago, however while walking idly along the streets in Galveston he had been attracted by music proceeding from a show tent, and went in. He found that a Dr. Arthur was giving hypnotic performances. He said that the hypnotic condition through which he was put left him in an exhausted condition, and though he desired to "quit" he could not do so; that he felt forced to attend the performances. He said he intended to request Dr. Arthur to release him from the influence.

The reporter asked Mr. Sterling if he had agreed to the proposed experiment by Mr. Witt voluntarily, and he replied that he had as an accommodation to Mr. Witt. The other subject, Mr. Boehm, was about 28 years of age, and a resident of Galveston. He also was a subject of Dr. Arthur's, having been discovered by him during one of the performances. He said that he had never been hypnotized before he came into contact with Dr. Arthur, and that the latter did not consider him a very good subject.

At this juncture the telegraph instrument began its ticking. Operator Nolley stated that Mr. Witt, at the other end, desired to know if everything was ready for the test. An affirmative was reply was sent, and in a few moments Mr. Sterling was requested to take his seat near the telegraph table. He did so, and amid the ticking of the instrument Operator Nolley repeated the following instructions:

"Mr. Witt says for you to assume a comfortable position." The subject fixed himself in the chair. "Close your eyes and roll your eyeballs upward," was the next order. The subject closed his eyes. "When I count five you will be fast asleep," came over the wire. Then Operator Nolley slowly repeated the numbers up to five. With each number the subject's head dropped lower and lower, and when "five" was announced, the head lay on the chest, the subject was breathing strenuously, and he was apparently fast asleep. The reporter lifted his eyelids and found the eyeballs fixed and apparently sightless.

The fact that the subject slept was telegraphed to the hypnotist-operator at the other end and the command came back, "You will sleep until I command you to awake." This was followed by the statement, "You will have no feeling whatever." In order to test the result of the last suggestion the reporter obtained a large pin and thrust it up to the head in various parts of the subject's anatomy. He did not pay the slightest heed or show the least discomfort at being thus used as a pincushion. Several of those present also stuck pins in the inert form and vigorously pinched him, but with the same result.

These facts having been communicated the

hypnotist telegraphed: "When I count five you will wake up and find your chair is red hot." When the numeral "three" was called the subject began to move uneasily in the chair and to commence feeling anxiously in the vicinity of his coat tails. When five was called he bounded out of the chair as though he had really come into contact with a red hot stove.

The subject was then commanded to wake up, and in a few moments he did so, rubbing his eyes vigorously. The reporter questioned him closely as to what impressions he had received, but he replied that he had not received any; all he remembered was the injunction to go to sleep.

Mr. Boehm, the other subject, was then called to take the chair. He did so, and the same instructions were given him over the wire. He followed them out to the extent of closing his eyes, but sleep did not follow. Several attempts were made, but in vain. The hypnotist could not get command. The latter then suggested that the experiment be tried over the phone. Boehm accordingly went to that instrument and held the receiver to his ear. In the stillness which prevailed the suggestions of the hypnotist were plainly heard by those standing near the phone. He was told to close his eyes and he replied that they were closed. He was ordered to sleep, and the suggestion was made that he could not open his eyes. "Oh yes, I have them open!" replied the subject as he blinked at the telephone. Then he turned from the instrument with the announcement that Mr. Witt was coming over to the office. A few moments afterward the door opened and Mr. Witt entered. Boehm was standing at

the extreme end of the room and about sixty feet from Witt as he came in. Naturally all eyes were fixed upon the latter. Boehm's included. Suddenly Witt threw out his hand in the direction of Boehm, and to the intense surprise of those present the latter started on a dead run for the hypnotist, his head thrown forward and his eyes wide open and fixed. The hypnotist lead him around like a magnet drawing a piece of steel, remarking meanwhile "that is the man who wouldn't be hypnotized by telegraph."

He then lead the subject up to within ten feet of Operator Nolley and pointed to the latter's face. The subject darted forward and put his face close to that of the startled operator.

"Try to get away from him," suggested Mr. Witt. Mr. Nolley backed away, turned round and started in various directions, but it was of no use, the subject followed him where-ever he went, with his face close to the operator's in the most embarrassing and ludicrous manner, while the latter called out desperately: "Call him off. Call him off." The hypnotist clapped his hands and Boehm resumed his normal condition.

A few moments afterward he again put Boehn to sleep in a chair, and in a trice had him rigid so that try as he would he could not budge an inch. In the same way speech was denied him. After being released from this condition, he was put into the cataleptic state, and his body stretched rigidly between two chairs. That being satisfactorily terminated the hypnotist turned to the other subject—Sterling. He inquired how he felt, and Sterling replied that he had a headache. He was put to sleep in an instant and told that when he awoke the pain would be gone. Upon awakening he stated that he was cured. The hypnotist then suggested that he was hungry, and immediately Sterling assumed a most lugubrious expression and began to assert that he was hungry.

"I am blooming hungry you know," he asseverated, with a broad English accent. "I'm starved. Give me something to eat, for Gawd's sake."

"What would you like to eat?" asked the hypnotist.

"A nice, blooming steak," was the response.

"Well, here it is," said Witt, handing the subject a wad of paper.

Sterling seized it and commenced to tear it to pieces with the ravenousness of a starved wolf. He chewed it with every mark of epicurean delight and when his mouth was full of paper the hypnotist suddenly recalled him back to the refinements of life. An expression of intense disgust upon the subject's face was as hilariously amusing it was genuine.

"You are a cat," suddenly said the hypnotist.

"Yes, I am a cat," replied Sterling.

"Then act like a cat" was the suggestion, and immediately the man dropped all fours and commenced to mewl, spit, and throw-up his back like a genuine "Tommy."

"There's a rat over there," said Witt, and with incredible speed the subject dashed in on all fours in the midst of numerous rolls of paper. He was pleased when he awoke to find where he was. This concluded the various exhibitions of Mr. Witt's hypnotic powers.

Mr. Witt stated to the reporter that he commenced the study of hypnotism under Dr. Arthur and had assisted the latter with some of his exhibitions. He stated that he had taken up the study with the purpose of using it only as a means of good and if he found that he could accomplish anything.

—*Dallas Morning News*
May 16, 1897

❖ ❖ ❖

Cured By
Christian Science
Letter From Mr. Wm. Lochridge Of Austin Detailing
His Remarkable Experience

CORSICANA- Capt. O.H. Earle, conductor on the Cotton Belt between here and Waco, who has for years been a sufferer from partial paralysis, has taken much interest in the reported cure of Wm. Lochridge of Austin by Christian Science methods, and in order to satisfy himself upon the subject addressed a letter to Mr. Lochridge. The reply which was received Saturday corroborates the reports that have been published, and as it is on a subject of unusual interest some extracts from the letter are given:

"Dear Sir: Mr. Edgar Nalle, my brother-in-law, referred your letter regarding my cure to me for answer and I take great pleasure in doing so, and I am happy to say to you that I am perfectly healed, since a few minutes past 7 o'clock last Monday morning and never felt better in all my life. I was healed by a Christian Science healer. I was stricken with paralysis on the 10th of April last and [remainder of article illegible]."

—*Dallas Morning News*
August 31, 1897

❖ ❖ ❖

Hypnotic Test

TURNER- Lawrence Kenner, a young railroad man, who possesses wonderful powers as a hypnotist, will undertake to hypnotize four subjects by telephone, he being in Houston Heights, the subjects at Turner, separated by a distance of several miles. After putting the subjects to sleep he will defy anyone to awaken them by the ordinary method. A committee of physicians have volunteered to witness the test and see that there is no trickery.

—*San Antonio Daily Light*

❖ ❖ ❖

For A Katy Ticket
A Mind Reader
Will Search The City.
Mr. Bass Has Announced For
A Novel Test Of Mind Reading
With Prof. Califf.

SAN ANTONIO- On Saturday of next week a novel test of mind reading will be given in this city in which a railroad ticket for a trip over the Katy Flyer from San Antonio to St. Louis will be offered as a prize. For some time past City Passenger and Ticket Agent G. J. Bass has been communicating with Prof. H. Califf, a noted mind reader, for the test, and yesterday he received a letter stating that he will be here next Saturday. Prof. Califf has given successful tests of mind reading throughout the country.

Mr. Bass has selected a number of well known business men of this city to act as a committee for the occasion. The committee will consist of T.L. Conroy, of the firm Conroy & Rice, Nat B. Washer, of Washer Bros. Chas, B. Mullaly, of the Carter Mullaly Transfer Company and W.T. Way, of the Strahorn-Hutton-Evans Commission Company. The test will consist of the finding of a railroad ticket good for a ride on the Katy Flyer from San Antonio to St. Louis and if Prof. Califf finds it it will be his property.

The committee will hide the ticket and Prof. Califf will be blindfolded to look for it. He will have sixteen thicknesses of black silk with cotton batting tied over his eyes and in that manner he will be sent out to find the ticket. He will be seated on a hack and blindfolded and will drive the horse while the committee will ride in the back to see that everything is carried on properly.

While it may seem hazardous for a man to drive through the streets blindfolded, it is said of Prof. Califf that he has done this in many cities throughout the north and east and has never as much as scratched the paint off a carriage in driving in that man-

ner, which appears to be a pretty good guarantee as to his ability to handle a team of horses blindfolded.

The committee will select a place for hiding the ticket by each member writing a place on a slip of paper which will be thrown into a hat. The name of the place selected from the hat will be the location for hiding the ticket. The committee will meet at the city ticket office of the M.K. & T., 131 Alamo plaza between 2 and 3 o'clock on the afternoon of Saturday March 3, for the purpose of hiding the ticket. After hiding it they will return to the ticket office and the hunt will begin. If Prof. Califf fails to find the ticket he is to defray all expenses connected with the test.

—*San Antonio Daily Light*
February 23, 1900

Think It Was A Miracle
Methodist Minister Recovers After Being Apparently Dead

BEEVILLE- Rev. W.C. Gadis, the aged Methodist minister of Clareville, who was restored to life after having been pronounced dead and his coffin sent for several nights ago, is reported to be improving. His peculiar restoration is attracting considerable attention and has been the subject to much comment during the past two or three days. Those who were attending his bedside say he was to all appearances as dead as ever man was and his restoration is looked upon by many as a miracle.

—*Dallas Morning News*
July 30, 1900

❖ ❖ ❖

Woman Guided By Dreams

Mrs. Moores Of Texarkana Recovers $2,800 That Was Buried During The Civil War

TEXARKANA- Students of psychic matters will find food for thought and refection in the following well authenticated experience of Mrs. Rachel P. Moores, one of Texarkana's oldest residents, a lady of education, refinement and wealth, and one of the leading members of the First Baptist Church.

Before the Civil War, and for several years thereafter, Mrs. Moores resided on her beautiful country plantation near Alamo Mills, about twenty miles south of Texarkana. They had been large slaveholders, and in the early part of 1866 had many of their former slaves living on the place with them. About that time several robberies by ex-slaves of their former masters were reported in this section, the news of which occurrences led to a consultation between Col. Moores and his wife as to the proper action necessary for the safety of their own money. It was decided best that the Colonel go alone, at night, and bury the treasure at some suitable and safe place. This was done. Eleven years later he died suddenly without acquainting his wife with the location of the hidden money, and after repeated efforts to find it the widow gave it up, after becoming convinced that it was lost forever so far as she was concerned. Some three or four moths ago Mrs. Moores' residence, a fine structure, situated on State Street, was burned by reason of which she became a heavy loser.

Her nerves were very much affected and she grieved continually. One night about a month ago she dreamed the hidden money was at a certain place on the old plantation, where it had been buried thirty-five years ago, and two nights later the vision in every detail was repeated.

She said nothing about this to even her most intimate friends, though every few nights the same dream visited her, each time describing vividly and minutely the place of the lost treasure. Mrs. Moores was not a believer in dreams and omens: she has never been reckoned as superstitious, yet the persistent recurrence of this vision caused her finally to resolve on an investigation. Quietly and without acquainting any of her purpose, she went about the work. She asked a male relative to go on a visit with her to the country, and about a week ago they landed at the old plantation. A negro man was employed and the three started out over the place, and, after several hours of wandering, the landmarks, as seen in Mrs. Moores dream, were found. After nearly an hour's digging he said it was no use, "dis groun' ain't never been 'sturbed sine de Lord mad it." But Mrs. Moores was not satisfied and she urged the negro to go on with the digging. After considerable parleying the work was resumed and at about the third stroke the spade struck a metal substance which [article ends].

—*Dallas Morning News*
January 7, 1901

❖ ❖ ❖

Extraordinary Story
Eggs Found At Blum And Bonham Foretell Judgment Day

BLUM- On Sunday, the 17th day of May, my little boy, aged 2 years, while passing through the yard noticed a peculiar looking egg in a hen's nest. He took the egg to his mother, and this is what she saw written on the egg in golden letters: "Behold, the Lord cometh." "Judgment is at hand." "Prepare to meet thy God."

These letters were not scratched on the shell, but raised and could be easily felt. At least a hundred people have seen this egg and will vouch for the truth of this statement. Is this not exactly what was on the Waco and Woodbary eggs? Can there be any satisfactory explanation given for this freak? Could this work be done by any chemical process? W.F. Lowe

BONHAM- A number of the colored folks of Bonham are wrought up over the reported appearance of a hen egg among one of them bearing the embossed inscription: "The end of the world is at hand." Some of them say they are not quite ready for that occasion.

—Dallas Morning News
May 20, 1903

❖ ❖ ❖

Queer Dream Preceded Death
Conductor Of Ill Fated Train Almost Persuaded To Lay Off

DENISON- A remarkable case of premo-nition of death through a dream has come to light in connection with the Katy collision near Ward. I.T. where Conductor Burekell was killed.

A few minutes before the collision occurred, Conductor Burekell told the story of his dream to Bob Duel, the fireman on the train. He also told it to others during the day. Conductor Burekell dreamed that he had gone to heaven, and that heaven was one end of his run. When he arrived there he found that he was fifteen times out and complained to the officials that he couldn't make any money that way. Trainmaster Gardner, Burekell dreamed, told him that it was all right and that he would draw straight time while he was in heaven. The dream made somewhat of an impression on the conductor and he almost made up his mind to lay off.

—Dallas Morning News
February 21, 1907

❖ ❖ ❖

Coffin Dream On Last Day

DALLAS- Fate seemed to stretch its shadow forward in the tragedy of little Donald Grant, Police Inspector Grant's only child, for it developed yesterday that the boy, who was killed by Jonathan Bulkley's automobile on Saturday afternoon on the morning of that same day had a dream that seemed almost a premonition of death. The climax of his vision, as he related it to his mother before going out for the playtime that was to be his last, was a glimpse of a small white coffin. With his sight of the coffin the dream ended, and the lad awoke in a depressed condition he could not shake off, even to please his mother. His sadness became so manifest that Mrs. Grant asked him at his late breakfast what ailed him. Donald, who was 8 years old, answered he had "an awful funny dream." "Funny" is boyland's adjective for everything unusual.

—*Dallas Morning News*
June 20, 1907

❖ ❖ ❖

Suggests
Hypnotic Spell
Man Who Suddenly Lost Power Of Speech And Hearing Comments On His Case

FORT WORTH- Frank Blocker, who suddenly lost his speech and hearing last Tuesday night, is now of the belief that he is under a hypnotic spell. Closest examination by physicians fails to disclose any disorders in the organs of the ears or throat, and the case is a complete mystery. There is a theory that Blocker is suffering from autohypnosis from observing a deaf-mute.

Blocker was a railway clerk on the Fort Worth and Denver working in the same car with his brother, A.B. Blocker. Another brother B.B. Blocker of Corpus Christi, upon reading the newspaper reports of the peculiar incident, came to Fort Worth and is the constant companion of his unfortunate brother, who is hopeful of regaining his speech and hearing.

—*Dallas Morning News*
February 8, 1910

Had Premonition Of Death
Henry Carter Harrison, McLennan County Farmer, Makes Will, Then Passes Away.

WACO- Henry Carter Harrison, a McLennan County farmer, aged 43, died to-day and will be buried to-morrow at Valley Mills, Bosque County. Mr. Harrison leaves a widow and three children. He was the grandson of Gen. James E. Harrison and grand nephew of Gen. Tom Harrison, both distinguished Confederate brigadiers, who are buried here.

Last week the deceased came to Waco and wrote his will, stating that his end was near at hand. He was suffering from a stroke of paralysis. Part of his estate is land, which is located near the famous Bosque Falls.

—*Dallas Morning News*
December 13, 1910

UFOs

Ball Of Fire

VERNON- At Vernon, while the lunar eclipse was in progress, a ball of fire about the size of a flour barrel fell. It emitted a blue blaze, and was some time in falling, and made the earth shake when it finally reached it.

—San Antonio Daily Light
July 16, 1888

❖ ❖ ❖

A Fragmented Aerolite

GRANDVIEW- Last night about 11 o'clock a party fishing on Chambers Creek perceived the elements and the earth round about them as bright and luminous as noonday splendor. In the mid-heavens

three extra large meteors were traversing the heavens in a northern direction. Just as they vanished and the iridescent beauty with them three heavy sounds, fiercer and nosier than the noisiest anvil firing were distinctly heard. Now the query: What is the truth of the phenomenon?

—Dallas Morning News
July 29, 1889

❖ ❖ ❖

A Phantom Airship
No Man Knows Its Whenceness Or Whither It Goeth

PARIS- As Dr. J. M. Stephens, a prominent physician of Paris, was going to Emerson, about ten miles north of the city, yesterday evening, he sighted a balloon several hundred feet in the air, drifting southward. He watched it a short time, when it disappeared in the clouds. He says it was a very large balloon, probably 100 feet in length, and that he could plainly see the car. As no one here knows of it ascension or has since heard from it, it has excited much curiosity.

—*Dallas Morning News*
September 18, 1889

❖ ❖ ❖

A Flying Meteor

SAN ANTONIO- Those of the citizens residing on East Commerce Street who happened to be looking in the right direction were treated to a splendid sight last evening at 8:15 o'clock. A brilliant meteor was observed shooting in a westerly direction at an apparently low elevation. It presented the appearance of a brilliant ball of fire of iridescent hues, changing from light green to rich orange and red. It threw off a train of brilliant sparks and remained in view for about one minute.

—*San Antonio Daily Light*
June 28, 1890

❖ ❖ ❖

A Ball Of Fire
Hanging Over The Town Of Bonham Several Nights In Succession

BONHAM- Last week parties in the northwest part of the city claimed to have seen for several nights in succession a large luminous ball resembling a meteor

save in speed. Every time it appeared above the horizon northwest of the city, passing slowly in a southwest direction, it would suddenly descend toward the earth and disappear.

Last night about 8:30 o'clock this same ball of fire passed over the northwestern part of the city, creating considerable excitement. People had a good view of it and watched it about ten minutes when it disappeared, seemingly in Powder Creek bottom. The ball looked as large as a man's fist. It had the brilliancy of the moon and was high up in the heavens, traveling slowly to the southwest, where it disappeared. Many residents of the northwestern part of the city saw it. Some looked with awe and superstition.

—*Dallas Morning News*
February 25, 1893

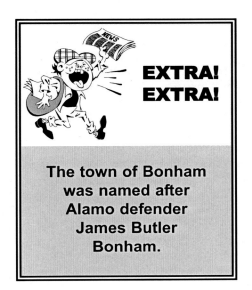

EXTRA! EXTRA!

The town of Bonham was named after Alamo defender James Butler Bonham.

HIDDEN HEADLINES of TEXAS

Struck By Lightning

SAN ANTONIO- During the thunder shower and electrical storm of Wednesday afternoon last, the cupola of the home of Mr. T.J. McMinn, on Lanrel Heights, was demolished by a bolt of lightning, which exhibited peculiar phenomena. After striking and twisting the cupola, the fluid set the wood-work afire, but the blaze was quickly extinguished. The family were sitting on the front gallery and a ball of fire, just as the stroke fell, ran past the front of the house. It is described as being about the size of a half bushel measure.

—*San Antonio Daily Light*
July 27, 1894

❖ ❖ ❖

A Huge Meteor

BRENHAM- At 5:40 o'clock this morning a large meteor passed over Brenham, going from northwest to southeast. In the wake of the meteor was a long track resembling smoke, which remained ten or fifteen minutes afterward and then gradually faded away.

The more ignorant of the negroes were very much alarmed at the unusual star and some of them thought the wavy line made by the meteor was writing and tried to decipher it. They claim it is the harbinger of disaster, citing the handwriting on the wall at the feast of Belshazzer as an instance of a similar nature.

—*Dallas Morning News*
May 26, 1895

M M T U W In Script

NAVASOTA- This morning at 5:30 people were startled by a loud report. The noise seemed to originate in the northwest and immediately across the heavens there extended a narrow line of smoke of dazzling whiteness so bright that it was painful to the eyes. Immediately it began to fade to the color of burning sulfur and spread out over the heavens in various colors—violet, purple, blue, then the script letters M M T U W formed and the heavens became clear.

Dozens of people saw it here and inquiries developed that it had been seen in parts of Brazos and Washington Counties. The negroes are very much frightened.

—*Dallas Morning News*
May 26, 1895

❖ ❖ ❖

That Wandering Airship
Was Seen At Denton As It Was Cavorting Through Space

DENTON- That Denton is not to be behind the other towns and cities in north Texas is shown by the fact that the mysterious airship of which so much has been said and written in the last few days has been seen here by at least two credible persons, one a gentlemen, the other a lady, whose reputations for truthfulness can not be assailed. The gentleman who saw the ship says that he was standing in his yard watching with the aid of a pair of powerful marine glasses the stars, when a shadow fell over the moon, obscuring it for a moment. The sky being cloudless, he looked to examine the cause. The lady mentioned is a member of the Ariel society, is one of the most widely read ladies in town, and is not one upon whose credibility anything of a hoax-like nature could be imposed, her description though much less explicit than the gentleman's as she was unaided by any glasses, tallies almost exactly with the above. When she saw it the ship was bounding along through space like a balloon.

—*The Galveston Daily News*
April 15, 1897

❖ ❖ ❖

Keeping People Awake

MEXIA- The account of the airship appearing in *The News* to-day created much excitement here. No doubt that many people will watch for its early appearance.

—*Dallas Morning News*
April 17, 1897

❖ ❖ ❖

Several See It
At Bonham

BONHAM- The mysterious airship passed over the northern part of this city last night at 3:15. John German, motor-man on the electric line, was returning to the city on his regular run. The car had slowed up as it was rounding the sharp curve just beyond Russell Heights, when Mr. German noticed a light moving rapid-ly form the southeast toward the north-west. At first he thought it was a shooting star and called the attention of several young men in the car to the phenomenon. All the parties pressed to the front of the car, and seeing that the light lingered longer than any shooting star they had ever seen, they brought the car to a standstill and all alighted to the ground in order to get a better view of the wonderful sight.

The moving light approached rapidly and as it passed north of them the light gleamed out brightly, looking as large as the bottom of a half-bushel measure, pierc-ing the dark ether with the brilliancy of the headlight of a railroad engine. Mr. German had not read of the mysterious air-ship and was gazing upon it with wonder and awe. He could hear a whizzing, whirring sound as it passed. It looked like it was about a quarter of a mile high. For about four minutes they watched the won-derful sight, when it disappeared in the northwest, going toward Denison.

Mr. Oscar Lusk was the only one in the crowd who had read of the wonderful air-ship, and he explained all he had read about it in *The News* and the mystery was cleared up satisfactorily to all, everyone agreeing that it was the wonderful aerial navigator. Messrs. Oscar Lusk, Will Pope and Sherwood Spotts were present with Mr. German and will vouch for the truth-fulness of his statement.

—*Dallas Morning News*
April 18, 1897

❖ ❖ ❖

A Windmill Demolishes It

AURORA- About 6 o'clock this morning the early risers of Aurora were astonished at the sudden appearance of the airship which has been sailing around the country. It was traveling due north and much nearer the earth than before. Evidently some of the machinery was out of order, for it was making a speed of only ten or twelve miles an hour, and gradually settling toward the earth. It sailed over the public square and when it reached the north part of town it collided with the tower of Judge Proctor's windmill and went into pieces with a terrific explosion, scattering debris over several acres of ground, wrecking the windmill and water tank and destroying the judge's flower garden. The pilot of the ship is supposed to have been the only one aboard and, while his remains were badly disfigured, enough of the original has been picked up to show that he was not an inhabitant of this world.

Mr. T.J. Weems, the U.S. Army Signal Service officer at this place and an authority on astronomy gives it as his opinion that the pilot was a native of the planet Mars. Papers found on his person—evidently the records of his travels—are written in some unknown hieroglyphics and cannot be deciphered. This ship was too badly wrecked to form any conclusion as to its construction or motive power. It was built of an unknown metal, resembling somewhat a mixture of aluminum and silver, and it must have weighed several tons. The town is to-day full of people who are viewing the wreckage and gathering specimens of strange metal from the debris. The pilot's funeral will take place to-morrow.

—*Dallas Morning News*
April 19, 1887

EXTRA! EXTRA!

Many researchers believe the body of the "extraterrestrial" is buried in Aurora Cemetery.

Airship Seen In Galveston

GALVESTON- Walter L. Norwood, an undertaker, viewed it yesterday morning.
—*The Galveston Daily*
News April 22, 1897

❖ ❖ ❖

Airship Photographed

GALVESTON- Peter Erhart of the Santa Fe general offices photographed the airship at 5:30 o'clock Sunday morning on

the country road. At least he has a photograph of what he says is the airship.
—*The Galveston Daily News*
April 27, 1897

❖ ❖ ❖

Another Airship

SAN ANTONIO- Conductor Sam Betters and Brakeman Harry Babcock of the Southern Pacific are of the opinion that there is a whole fleet of air ships wandering about in the skies, or that the one particular airship, which nearly everybody claims to have seen at another place at the same time is a fast traveler. As Messers. Betters and Babcock were out on their run Monday night, Babcock was sitting in the brake of a box car while the train was passing Spofford. The train was speeding along, when something struck Babcock on the shoulder and almost knocked him from his perch. He only heard a humming noise and as he turned to see where the mysterious blow came from he saw the white-winged air ship making fast time for the west.
—*San Antonio Daily Light*
April 29, 1897

❖ ❖ ❖

Airship

SAN ANTONIO- Sheriff R.W. Dome is in receipt of numerous communications from afar about the recent airship he saw, an account of which as published in The Express.
—*San Antonio Daily News*

May 10, 1897
Airship

GALVESTON- The Nashville airship being an actuality seems to create very little interest. The airship that the people demand is a cigar-shaped affair that runs in a southwesterly direction at night.
—*The Galveston Daily News*
May 12, 1897

❖ ❖ ❖

Phenomenon In The Sky

GLIDDEN– Railroad men coming out of Glidden to San Antonio report a phenomenon in the sky, which is visible about 4 o'clock in the morning. It is a large star due south, which, they say, changes colors. The varying colors are red, white, and blue. Those who claim they have seen it are Conductor Cal Warner, Engineer Walter Jordon and Fireman Ed Stevens, of the Southern Pacific. None of these gentlemen touch liquor of any kind, and none of them are active members of any prevaricating sect, and they do not believe that is it an optical illusion that causes this strange vision. They say the star changes colors like a flash of light and they observe it on every trip as they leave Glidden.
—*San Antonio Daily Light*
December 20, 1897

❖ ❖ ❖

HIDDEN HEADLINES of TEXAS

Aerial Phenomena

SHERMAN- George Campbell, aged 12 years, son of E.W. Campbell, who lives just north of the city on the "Eighty-foot" road, was a witness to a startling phenomenon last night shortly after 9 o'clock.

He is a bright, intelligent little fellow, who said he didn't believe in ghosts: that his parents had never scared him with spook stories, and he is one of the best behaved scholars in the fourth grade at the Franklin school building. His story as told to a News reporter to-day is as follows:

"Last night papa and I were riding along in the "Eighty-foot" road, about two and a half miles north of town, when all at once everything got very bright. We saw a great ball of fire coming down toward the ground. It got within about three feet of the ground and seemed to rest for a while and then it went back up until it got velar out of sight. There was a buzzing sound all the time."

George describes it as being about ten feet in diameter and that it hurt one's eyes to look at it. Although they were very close to it, he says that he did not feel any heat. The point at which the strange light descended is rather low and swampy. The fact that a rather low registration of the barometer has prevailed for the past few days may furnish to the scientific an explanation.

—*Dallas Morning News*
October 5, 1898

❖ ❖ ❖

EXTRA! EXTRA!

Strange sightings still continue today, as each year hundreds of UFOs are reported from witnesses who have seen something unknown in the Texas sky.

Aerial Phenomena In Texas

GARLAND- A remarkable aerial phenomenon was witnessed last night at 9 o'clock by the people of Garland and vicinity which affords much food for thought among astronomers and scientists. In this hour of unrest such an omen will be observed and hailed with delight by both army and navy, as it is a well known fact that superstition lurks upon shipboard as well as in the trenches.

A meteor descended from a point neat the sky's center, traveling slowly in an easterly direction, suddenly changed its course and shot upwards, when it burned, throwing into the air three distinct bodies, each taking its own course. The first of them was a bright red, the second a white light and the third a bright blue. The red and blue lights soon died out, but the white one continued on its way a few seconds when it burst, emitting a shower of stars which were extinguished almost immediately.

—*Dallas Morning News*
October 5, 1898

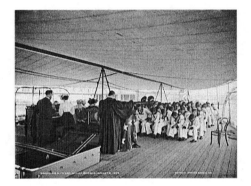

Brilliant Meteor
At Austin

AUSTIN- At about 9:30 to-night outdoor folks were startled by a brilliant meteor that illuminated the city for a few seconds almost as light as day. It traveled in a southwesterly direction and exploded with a loud report over the western part of the city, startling the people, who imagined dynamite or a steam boiler had exploded. Messages were sent to police headquarters to learn the facts. Scores of people saw it, some estimating its size as large as that of a sugar hogshead.

—*Dallas Morning News*
August 24, 1900

Rainbow At Night
Remarkable Phenomenon
Witnessed By People At Terrell

TERRELL- The phenomenon of a rainbow at night was seen by Terrell people last night. A black cloud lay in the west and a full moon shone in the east. The reflection produced a genuine rainbow that executed the curiosity of many who had never witnessed such a freak before.

—*Dallas Morning News*
August 2, 1901

❖ ❖ ❖

Meteor Seen
At San Antonio
Instead Of Dipping Toward The
Earth It Went Upward

SAN ANTONIO- A meteor of unusual size and exceeding brilliancy was seen in the heavens over the northern part of the city at 7 o'clock this evening, and it remained in sight about half a minute. Instead of dipping toward the earth, the meteor took an upward turn, going in a northwest course, leaving in its trail a perfect shower of sparks. When first seen it had a long tail and greatly resembled a comet.

—*Dallas Morning News*
May 14, 1902

❖ ❖ ❖

HIDDEN HEADLINES of TEXAS

An Immense Meteor Frightens Many Texans
Viewed In Weatherford, Wichita Falls And Mineral Wells With Much Appearance Of Big Sky Rocket, Is Accompanied By Hissing And Roaring Sounds.

WEATHERFORD- About 6:30 o'clock this morning a monster meteor passed over the city, creating a glare in the heavens that was sufficient to light up rooms brilliantly in which the shades had been drawn over the windows. The meteor seemed to pass from the southwest in a northeasterly direction and its appearance upon the southwest horizon was characterized by a great noise as of distant thunder.

Hundreds of people in this city witnessed the phenomenon, and those who were out attending to their stock at that time say the animals all seemed to cower in the most abject fear.

—*Dallas Morning News*
December 15, 1908

❖ ❖ ❖

Looked As Big As Moon
DENTON- A meteor, apparently as big as the moon, was observed here this morning about 6 o'clock. It was bright enough to cast a shadow. Observers say small particles were continually breaking away from the parent body during the flight which appeared on the northwestern horizon and disappeared in the southeast.

—*Dallas Morning News*
December 15, 1908

Seen By Sherman People

SHERMAN- An unusually brilliant and in other respects-peculiar meteor-phenomenon was witnessed about 6:30 o'clock in the low western skies. The street light of the aerial visitor grew dully red and the moon light was shadowy in comparison.

—*Dallas Morning News*
December 15, 1908

❖ ❖ ❖

Strange Light In The Sky

HILLSBORO- A number of citizens of Hillsboro observed during the early portion of last night what appeared to be a large balloon passing over the city, its course being from a northwesterly direction. What is supposed to have been the light in the car is said to have been distinctly discernible, some of the observers at first taking it to be a meteor, but a closer view developed what resembled the large, inflated body of a balloon, and it was watched until it passed out of sight.

—*Dallas Morning News*
March 24, 1909

❖ ❖ ❖

Meteor Startles West Texas Towns
Turns Night Into Day At 10:05 P.M. Rumbles. Explodes. Makes Earth Quake.

DUBLIN- A large meteor passed over the city to-night at 10:05. The heavens were lighted up as bright as day for about a minute and was immediately followed by a terrific explosion, which shook the earth as if by an earthquake. Windows and the iron awnings about the city rattled as if shaken by some unseen power.

The meteor came from the northeast and traveled in a southwesterly direction. A pin could have been picked up on the street, so bright was the light. The time from passing of the meteor until the explosion was about one minute.

—*Dallas Morning News*
May 31, 1909

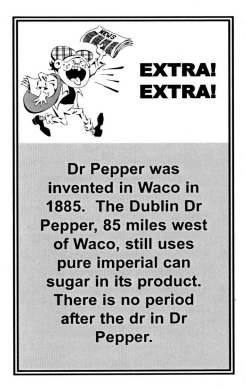

**EXTRA!
EXTRA!**

Dr Pepper was invented in Waco in 1885. The Dublin Dr Pepper, 85 miles west of Waco, still uses pure imperial can sugar in its product. There is no period after the dr in Dr Pepper.

Brilliancy Of Arc Light

CLEBURNE- Price Allard observed the large meteor speeding across the sky last night at 10 o'clock, and stated that it had the brilliancy of an arc of light. The memorial service in honor of Bishop Galloway had just closed at the Main Street Methodist Church, and many people were compelled to look upward when the brilliant ball suddenly appeared and rushed with the speed of a cannon ball to the tree-top horizon. Even after it was hidden from view the reflection was noticeable.

—*Dallas Morning News*
June 1, 1909

Ennis People
See Meteor

ENNIS- A large meteor of transcendent brilliancy sped across the heavens from southwest to northeast about 10 o'clock last night. It was seen by many people and was a grand sight. It caused timid people to quake with superstitious awe. The body of the meteor was followed by a waving blaze, apparently twenty-five or thirty feet in length, and created a light that far out-shone the brightness of a full moon. Persons who witnessed the phenomenon say they heard three distinct explosions or intonations as the blazing star passed below the horizon.

—*Dallas Morning News*
September 30, 1909

INDEX
LISTED BY TEXAS TOWNS

HIDDEN HEADLINES of TEXAS

HIDDEN HEADLINES of TEXAS

PAGE 154

HIDDEN HEADLINES of TEXAS

HIDDEN HEADLINES of TEXAS

HIDDEN HEADLINES of TEXAS

HIDDEN HEADLINES of TEXAS

HIDDEN HEADLINES of TEXAS

About the Author

Chad Lewis is a paranormal investigator for Unexplained Research LLC, with a Master's Degree in Applied Psychology from the University of Wisconsin-Stout. Chad has spent years traveling the globe researching ghosts, strange creatures, crop formations, werewolves, and UFOs. Chad is a former State Director for the Mutual UFO Network and has worked with BLT Crop Circle Investigations. Chad is the organizer of *The Unexplained* Conferences and the host of *The Unexplained* paranormal radio talk show. He is the co-author of the *Road Guide to Haunted Locations* series.

HIDDEN HEADLINES

Strange, Unusual, & Bizarre
Newspaper Stories 1860-1910

Hidden Headlines
of
WISCONSIN
Researched and Compiled by
Chad Lewis
Foreword by Michael Bie
ISBN-13: 978-0-9762099-8-0

Hidden Headlines
of
NEW YORK
Researched and Compiled by
Chad Lewis
Foreword by Linda Moulton Howe
ISBN-13: 978-0-9762099-9-7

Hidden Headlines
of
CALIFORNIA
Researched and Compiled by
Chad Lewis